ENOUGH

ABOUT

GRAMMAR

WHAT REALLY MATTERS
AND WHAT REALLY DOESN'T

Joe Floren

Illustrations by Michael Frary

TWAIN PRODUCTIONS, PUBLISHERS
WHEATON, ILLINOIS

TO OBTAIN OTHER TWAIN PRODUCTS TO HELP YOU WRITE BETTER WITH LESS
WHEEL-SPINNING, YOU MAY USE THE ORDER FORM PROVIDED AT THE BACK OF
THE BOOK

For

HULDA MARIE CARLSON FLOREN

who, a long time ago, probably had
something to do with this

the <u>Mark</u> of exceptional writing instruction
2120 Timberlane
Wheaton, Illinois 60187
630/665-9370

CONTENTS

A friend who plays guitar for round-the-campfire singalongs likes to warm up shy participants by saying:

"Now, remember: If you're gonna sing, you have to risk being heard."

It's that way with writing. When you write, you have to risk being read. And that alone is often enough to cause paralysis, procrastinating and panic. Is it the fear of exposing your ideas to criticism or ridicule? No, you express your ideas daily in conversation.

It is, rather, the absolute terror of committing a Grammatical Mistake.

Two things most often impair a person's ability to write. One is the tendency to be wordy and rambling. The other is lack of basic grammatical skill.

The two differ in an important way:

Wordy, disorganized writers usually don't recognize these problems, and write in spite of them. But people who have poor grammar, or--the huge majority--those who *think* they have, cringe at putting anything at all onto paper.

From four decades of conducting writing workshops, I've found that the typical educated adult is like a person in the Fun House, looking first into the fat mirror and then into the skinny mirror. Both images, of course, are distortions. Most people have trouble seeing their own wordiness; at the same time, most have a grossly exaggerated view of themselves as grammatical dunces.

Whom to thank for this misperception? The responsibility must be laid mainly at the feet of teachers. Teachers who, over eight, 12, 16 years of schooling us, not only condoned but actually encouraged verbosity. (Schoolroom Memory #1: Remember the best grades for the longest papers? The gold star for spelling the most obscure words? How many teachers have you known--in your whole life--who encouraged conciseness?)

Rewarding wordy habits is one side of the coin. The other is early and continuous criticism for seemingly--and truly--minor points of usage. (Schoolroom Memory #2: Recall the red checkmark? How long did it continue? High school? College? Tell me those "awk's" and "frag's" on your grad-school papers weren't written in red.)

But jobs do require writing. And most of it must be done, however reluctantly, by checkmark-scarred writers like you, and--the ultimate ego test--often submitted for review.

All it takes is for your first editor to wield that red pencil (it *is* red, isn't it?) with a particularly heavy hand, and you may well go sit in the corner, assume the fetal position, and suck your thumb.

Take heart. Odds are, you are underrating yourself, overrating the problem. Even though you can't recite the rules, you follow most of them. And the others--the ones that matter--are fewer and easier to learn than you expect.

And remember:

✏ *You are not alone.* "Common grammatical errors" means just what it says. Most people have at least some trouble with punctuation, capitalization, usage--certainly spelling. Few writers, even professionals, can produce a message of any length totally free of usage errors. Big-company advertisements, newspaper columns, television scripts, professional brochures contain errors ranging from funny to glaring. Of course they shouldn't. Of course they do. (This book has many examples--from the writing of experts as well as novices; you won't have to look far to find others.)

✏ *Grammar is imperfect,* full of holes, a swiss cheese. Most rules have exceptions; most exceptions themselves call for exceptions. Few definitions fit every time. Many of the rules have been ignored for decades by competent writers who have seen them, correctly, as irrelevant and cramping.

☞ *Grammar is subjective*. Grammar texts frequently disagree--on definitions, on how strictly a given rule should be observed. Experts on the subject quarrel; whole books have been written to debate individual usage preferences.

☞ *Few bosses are skilled editors,* other than those trained for an editing job. Most reviewers of employees' written work have inherited the editorial eyeshade along with other hats, as a result of a promotion. Most are not especially verbally trained, nor do they spend much time improving their knowledge of language. Many are only fair writers. Some read very little. They are far more likely to nitpick small errors than they are to detect major ones or understand writing principles.

Most of them mean well.

☞ *Grammar is changing*. What counts as good usage varies from year to year.

☞ *Some things matter; some don't*. This book will focus on those that do, discard those that don't--and help you tackle your writing job with confidence.

It will tell you enough about grammar.

MEMORIES OF ENGLISH 101

Getting Squared Away

CHAPTER 1

Stumbling Blocks to Stepping Stones

Mr. Language Person is the creation of Dave Barry, a humorous columnist as well as a humor columnist. Mr. L. P. periodically gives grammar and related (and unrelated) advice in a Q-and-A format. A sample:

> *"Q. Dear Mr. Language Person:*
> *Like many people, I often get confused as to when to use 'affect' and when to use 'infect.' Can you help me out?*
>
> "A. Here is a simple pneumatic device for telling these two similar-sounding words (or 'gramophones') apart. Just remember that 'infect' begins with 'in,' which is also how 'insect' begins, while 'affect' begins with 'af,' which is an abbreviation for 'Air Force.'"

This typical example is hilarious--yet sad. Hilarious because it is ridiculous; sad because it is no more ridiculous than many of the grammar rules to which students are exposed.

For instance, this rule is lifted verbatim from a book on my desk, on grammar for adults. You'll find the rule in any grammar text you own, I suspect in the same finger-waggling language:

> Remember (*waggle*), the subject of an infinitive is always in the objective case.

Is this advice correct? Yes. Then why is it ridiculous? Because it is a very complicated way to prevent a very unlikely error, that of saying, for instance:

> Did you want I to do it?

First off, almost no one but a Martian learning to speak Earthish would say *Did you want I to do it?* or *Would you like I to show you our spaceship?* So the rule is nearly unnecessary.

Secondly, anyone language-limited enough to say *Did you want I to do it?* is hardly likely to master the complexity of *The subject of an infinitive is in the objective case.* She would first have to remember what an infinitive is, then what case is, then what *objective* means--and relate all this to the particular sentence she is about to commit. So the rule is nearly unworkable.

Don't get me wrong.

I am not anti-rules, be they traffic signs or language guides. But rules and definitions should be as few as possible, and they should be clear and sensible.

A Stop sign at a busy intersection makes sense. A sign in mid-block of a two-way street telling you Do Not Drive in Reverse Gear in the Left Hand Lane is of doubtful value (and may even cause you to steer into someone's Winnebago while you read it).

It makes sense--it is necessary--to define and understand noun, verb, subject, clause and a handful of other language concepts. But it is pointless to have students recite what a compound-complex sentence is. It is of no value whatsoever for the typical writer to be able to define an indirect object. Think: *In what conceivable way might you write differently for knowing these things?* Ask your closest English teacher. Be prepared for a blank stare.

Some people like bright clothing; some prefer muted shades. But our lives would not be improved by our having to learn a name for each of these types--the "vividians" and the "blandinas," perhaps. That is, we could go on naming traits and subtraits endlessly.

It's probably okay for grammarians to label language thoroughly. It is their field; every field has to have its jargon--excuse me, nomenclature. But it serves little purpose for educators to pass on all these terms in class without thinking whether each is (a) needed (b) clearly understood (c) sensible. But they do.

"The subject of a clause," another book says, "is the thing that is being spoken of." In *The boy saw the dog*, the subject is *boy*. In *The dog was seen by the boy*, the subject becomes *dog*. Are we suddenly speaking of something different? Not so you'd notice. In *All of the leprechauns sang at once*, the subject is *all*. Ask a young student what is "being spoken of?" If he says *all* and not *leprechauns*, I will buy yez some Irish stew.

"A preposition," the rulebook goes on, "links a noun to some other part of the sentence." Yes--but so do other parts of speech. In the sentence *The buzzer startled Willie*, the word *startled* links the noun *buzzer* to the noun *Willie*. So is it a preposition? No, it is a verb.

One more, and I'll stop: "An adverb answers the questions Where, When," etc. Take the sentence: *On your visit, you will enjoy the*

2

splendor that is Spiraeus today and all the ruins there. In it, *today* tells "when" and *there* tells "where." Ah; they are adverbs, yes? Nah; they are adjectives, no.

In 40-plus years of Fortune 500 corporate editing, communications management, free-lance writing, and conducting thousands of writing workshops, I've learned a simple truth about grammar:

Some things matter; some don't.

The ones that matter, matter a great deal; this book will treat them very thoroughly. Most of those that don't aren't worth mentioning. Others deserve a few words explaining why they don't.

To benefit from this book, you will have to learn 12 grammatical terms.

Just a dozen. Not 112. Not 1200. Twelve are all that matter. But they matter a great deal. For emphasis, each of those terms will be circled thus ⬭ clause ⬭ when first introduced or occasionally when cross-referenced.

Although this is a book on correct usage--and thus in a sense a reference book--it also has become, as it has taken shape, a blueprint for writing well. As it progresses, you'll find in it a set of principles that will do two things: Make your writing more correct, and at the same time make it easier and more enjoyable to read.

I have no name for this dual-purpose recipe. But I have one for its outcome: Straightforward Writing.

Straightforward Writing has five principles. The first two are:

> **STRAIGHTFORWARD WRITING IS:**
>
> ➡ **DRIVEN BY CLAUSES**
> ➡ **POWERED BY ACTIVE VERBS**

Don't worry if those terms aren't familiar. We'll define them later. For now, just lean back and "feel" what clause-driven, active verb-powered writing can do:

> The <u>misapprehension</u> that American automobile design <u>skill is</u> a thing of the past <u>can be corrected</u> by a current survey of the work of Detroit designers. (*Two clauses, no active verbs.*)

> <u>If you think</u> <u>Detroit has lost</u> the touch, <u>you haven't looked</u> lately at what its <u>designers are doing</u>. (*Four clauses, four active verbs.*)

Notice the fast. gripping movement in this portion of a newspaper feature article. It is driven by clauses--noun/verb clusters; its five lines contain a dozen of them (underlined).

> Gary Robinson died hungry. He wanted fried chicken, the three-piece box for $2.19. Drunk, loud and obnoxious, he pushed ahead of seven customers in line at a fast-food chicken outlet. The counter girl told him that his behavior was impolite. She calmed him down with sweet talk, and he agreed to step to the end of the line. His turn came just before closing time, just after the fried chicken ran out.
>
> He punched the counter girl so hard her ears rang, and a security guard shot him--three times.   (Edna Buchanan)

Okay, so clause-carried writing moves fast. But doesn't this speed work against beauty or lyricism? Isn't the reader carried along too fast to stop and smell the daisies, as it were?

Well, let's see:

> The Lord is my shepherd; I shall not want;
> He maketh me to lie down in green pastures;
> He leadeth me beside the still waters; He restoreth my soul;
> He leadeth me in the paths of righteousness for his name's sake.
> Yea, though I walk through the valley of the shadow of death,
> I will fear no evil; for Thou art with me;
> Thy rod and thy staff they comfort me.
> Thou preparest a table before me in the presence of mine enemies;
> Thou anointest my head with oil; my cup runneth over.
> Surely goodness and mercy shall follow me all the days of my life;
> And I will dwell in the house of the Lord forever.

Fifteen clauses, 13 active verbs (no passives)--and lovely writing, even in translation.

If the war that began in 1776 was Revolutionary, so was the writing of Thomas Paine, whose booklet "Common Sense" played a large part in stirring the colonists to rebellion. Here is a segment which, although its style is formal, is--one commentator notes--"driven by a forward-moving energy." That energy owes much to its clause emphasis:

> O ye that love mankind! Ye that dare oppose, not only the tyranny, but the tyrant, stand forth! Every spot of the old world is overrun with oppression. Freedom hath been hunted round the globe. Asia and Africa have long expelled her. Europe regards her like a stranger, and England hath given her warning to depart. O receive the fugitive, and prepare in time an asylum for mankind.

4

fugitive, and <u>prepare</u> in time <u>an asylum</u> for mankind.

Ten clauses. Ten active verbs.

This book may be used in three ways:

❋ Most important, it provides a system of writing unlike any you have ever learned. Its five Principles of Straightforward Writing will help you write not only more clearly but also with fewer errors. Not every guidebook does that.

Some things that make your writing clearer (colloquial language, perhaps) may cause usage errors. Some things that help you write precisely correct prose (like skill with complex language) may cause you to write in a hard-to-read manner (by showing off that complexity.) This book will reduce your errors *and* increase your clarity. In the process you will also learn to write with both speed and style.

❋ It is a thoroughly indexed reference of specific usage issues and guidelines for solving them. These are not classic textbook problems, but the gritty ones of real life, those that cause grief for real on-the-job writers--as I have supervised them at work or observed them in classes for over four decades.

The guidelines will be explained with no grammatical jargon. Some rules are arbitrary; some are well-reasoned. I'll try to sort them out, and explain the reasons for the latter.

❋ You've probably been exposed to textbook grammar. If you have, and if some of its terms linger in your mind, this book gives you a useful cross-reference. First, its Index includes traditional grammatical language as well as terms unique to the book. Second, each major concept will be accompanied by a GRAMMATICALLY SPEAKING box, showing which traditional terms relate to that concept. If these boxes are not helpful, you are free--no, encouraged--to ignore them.

> **GRAMMATICALLY SPEAKING**
>
> A verb that conveys action is called a **transitive** verb. One that does not is called an **intransitive** verb.

Too often, it seems to me, the tone of grammar books carries at least the suggestion that the world of writing is booby-trapped, and that the writer can no sooner put pen to page than he/she will set off an error blast. Some grammar texts resemble giant dictionaries of faults, with giveaway subtitles (1064 Common Misspellings, Frequently Misused Words, Typical Causes of Verb Errors, etc.) from which the writer is encouraged to pick and choose.

"English usage is sometimes more than mere taste, judgment and education--sometimes it's sheer luck, like getting across the street."

--E. B. White

5

Your errors are largely minor, and easier to correct than you expect. I didn't say effortless. I said easier.

Yes, you are probably gun-shy. We'll fix that.

Most of all, it is not true that writing creatively and writing correctly collide. This book's systematic approach to Straightforward Writing will bring about more-correct writing. Conversely, your grasp of the grammar principles that matter will smooth your style and help you free your true self on paper.

This book seeks to present grammar as it always should have been presented--as a stepping stone rather than a stumbling block. I'll do my level best.

Joe Floren

CHAPTER 2

Pay Yer Money and Take Yer Choice

As a student sweats out a really rough test, many thoughts cross his mind, some unrelated to the questions being asked. One has to do with revenge; it is the dream, the fantasy, of someday reversing the roles and putting the teacher through a test. ("I'll show **you** a fused genitive participial referent, you. . .mutter, mutter. . .)

I recently had a chance to live that fantasy dream.

It came about by accident, not by design. While I drafted this book, I kept coming across examples of English usage that seemed not to fit the definitions I had learned. To double-check my understanding, I sought a professional second opinion--several second opinions.

My expert "panel" comprised two university professors of English, one English professor from a community college, and a high-school English teacher. Each was recommended by his or her department as the school's top grammarian. In addition I took advantage of two of the many "grammar hotlines" offered by universities through the country. The teachers accepted my nominal consulting payment. The hotline people worked free; my only cost was the phone call.

They all meant well, as did I.

I gave each one five sentences that I was unable to explain grammatically, and asked specific questions about each. These were not long or complex, but everyday sentences I had found myself saying or heard others around me say.

The sentences were:

> We went camping every summer.
> Shame on you, Watson, you bad dog!
> Let's go.
> The corn grows tall here.
> When I was in Alaska, I heard from my brother in Utah.

The results were astounding, and discouraging. *The experts disagreed on every example, sometimes giving me widely differing answers.* Some included complex grammatical reasons. Two noted that they had conferred with other teachers to assure correct answers.

The following pages summarize the examples, the questions I posed, and the gist of the answers. I have reconstructed the hotline responses from my phone notes; the four teachers' comments are excerpted but verbatim.

If your knowledge of grammar is fading or imperfect (join the crowd), you may not understand all the terms here. Don't let that stop you; *these pages are must reading.* Notice the wide range of responses--from experts on the subject:

1. He went camping every summer.

*Q. What part of speech is **camping,** and what if anything does it modify?*

* ❈ **Camping** is part of the verb **go camping**. It does not modify anything.
* ❈ **Camping** is a participle modifying **went.**
* ❈ **Camping** is an adverb modifying **went**. Although it looks like a gerund or a participle, here the function is clearly adverbial.
* ❈ **Camping** is a gerund, receiving the action of **go**.
* ❈ **Camping** is the object of the verb **went.**
* ❈ **Go camping** is a verb.

*Q. What role does the noun **summer** play in the sentence?*

* ❈ **Summer** is a noun functioning as an adverb.
* ❈ Prepositionally, the phrase would be (**in the**) **summer**. **Summer** is thus the object of a suppressed preposition.
* ❈ **Summer,** a noun-looking word, is clearly an adverb.
* ❈ **Every summer** is an adverbial phrase, but it is somewhat ambiguous whether it modifies **went** or **camping.**
* ❈ **Every summer** isn't anything grammatically.
* ❈ A case may be made for **every summer** being an adjective modifying **camping**, describing what kind of camping (that is, **every summer camping.**)

2. Shame on you, Watson, you bad dog!

Q. What is the verb?

* ❈ The verb is probably the subjunctive **be**; but the verb has been deleted.
* ❈ **Shame** is the verb. The unexpressed sentence is **I shame you.**

Q. What is the subject?

* ❈ **Shame** is the subject of this idiomatic expression.
* ❈ There is no verb and therefore no subject. It is not a sentence.
* ❈ It is a fragment, not a sentence. To consider it grammatically you must flesh it out: **I call down shame on you, Watson, you bad dog!**

Volunteered comments:

* ❈ **Shame** is not the subject; a noun, it is the direct object complement of

the implied phrasal verb **call down.** **(I call down shame on you....)**
❋ **Shame** is in a direct-address case. (**I put shame on you**, or **shame be on you**.)

*Q. How do you describe **Watson, you bad dog?***

❋ **Watson** is a vocative (a name, such as **O, Lord!**)
❋ It is a vocative followed by two more appositives.
❋ **Watson** is a noun of address. **You bad dog** is a second noun of address.
❋ **Watson** is an appositive, preceding the suppressed clause **you (are a) bad dog! You** is the subject of that clause.

3. Let's go.

Q. What is the subject?

❋ The subject of the verb **let** is **us**-- it is in the objective case.
❋ This is a tough one. The subject of the verb **let go** is **you.**
❋ The subject of the verb **let** is **you,** understood.
❋ The subject is **we** (substituted for **us).**
❋ **Let's go (let us go)** is an imperative. Its subject is **you. Us** is the object of the verb.

Q. What is the verb?

❋ **Let** is the verb. **Us go** is an infinitive phrase functioning as the direct object of the verb **let**; that is **(let us [to] go).**
❋ **Let go** is the verb. The noun **us** is object of a prepositional phrase, although there is no preposition expressed.
❋ **Go** is the verb. It's not grammatically clear what **let** is.

4. The corn grows tall here.

*Q. What part of speech is **tall**, and what does it modify? How about **here?***

❋ **Tall** is a predicate adjective that modifies **corn.** **Here** is an adverb of place modifying **grows.**
❋ This one was easy. **Tall** and **here** are adverbs describing how and where the corn grows.
❋ **Tall** is the predicate adjective complement of **grows.** **Here** is an adverb modifying **grows.**
❋ Both are adverbs. (This answer from two respondents.)

5. When I was in Alaska, I heard from my brother in Utah.

*Q. The first prepositional phrase, **in Alaska,** seems to modify the verb **was.** The second one, **in Utah**, seems to modify the noun **my brother.** Yet both appear to answer the adverbial question "where?" But an adverb can't modify a noun, like **brother**--or can it?*

❋ **In Alaska** is an adverbial phrase modifying **was.** **In Utah** is a reduced adjective clause modifying **brother**, i.e. **(who was) in Utah** became in Utah.
❋ **In Alaska** is an adverb modifying **was.** **In Utah** is an adjective modifying

NOTHING BRINGS BACK BAD schoolroom memories like being near someone who got an "A" in English and won't let you forget it.

brother, since it identifies **brother**.

❋ The phrase **in Alaska** is the object of the verb **was**. The phrase **in Utah** is the object of the entire last part of the sentence.

❋ **In Utah** is an adverb.

❋ **In Alaska**, a prepositional phrase, modifies **was**. **In Utah** is another prepositional phrase, but in this case it functions as an adjective by describing which brother.

*{This last answer, I suspect, is a correct one. But hold on---something seems backward about the reasoning here, a matter of fitting the question to the answer: **Modifying a noun, the word is an adjective; therefore it must answer the question "Which brother?"** A bright student may have instead reasonably concluded that it answers the adverbial question "Where?" If "in Alaska" describes "Where?" he might well ask, why would "in Utah" suddenly describe "Which brother?" The answer: Mostly because the textbook authors say it does.}*

6. That's not English the way I was taught it. *(This question asked of only three experts.)*

Q. *Is it possible for the passive verb to take a direct object? It seems to, in this example.*

❋ No, it cannot. Only an active verb can take a direct object. **It** here is a modifier of the verb **taught**.

❋ Yes, it can. The passive verb can take a direct object. This often occurs with ditransitive verbs, those that take both direct and indirect objects.

❋ **It** is a retained object. The sentence is elliptical. The full sentence would be **That is not English according to the way in which I was taught it.** Now all is clear. A retained object is identified by understanding the active verb construction from which the passive is derived

Over the telephone, the Q-and-A feature became interactive. "You've given me some real stumpers," one faculty person chided. I said I supposed so; had they been easy, I might have figured them out myself. (He had been called to the phone by a grad student who was manning--womaning, rather--the hotline. Her response to my first sentence: "Could you maybe give me a different example?")

The instructor, whose field, he said, was descriptive linguistics, was helpful and frank. "It's really hard to impose grammar rules onto real-life sentences," he explained.

Then why do examples in textbooks all work out perfectly? Obviously because the authors invent only ones that do--examples that make grammar look infallible. Learning to diagram contrived sentences and then realizing this system won't work in real life is like learning Spanish, then going to Mexico and not being able to order a glass of water or make change.

11

"My Lord, I do here complain that our language is extremely imperfect; and that the pretenders to polish and refine it have chiefly multiplied its abuses and absurdities."
--Jonathan Swift

"It's hard when you impose rigid grammar on a living language," he went on, candidly. "Rules don't necessarily hold true in usage."

Then, shouldn't students be told just that? That grammar is *not* infallible; that it *doesn't* always work; that some exceptions *can't* be explained. But that we are all doing the best we can; and we're better off with even an imperfect understanding than none at all.

Having been told that, honestly--having been dealt with straight--perhaps the student who can't make sense of a given rule might feel a little less dumb.

What to make of these divergent responses? Let me put it this way:

Let's assume that only one of the answers in each case is the correct one. Let's assume further that these experts--chosen by their schools--*are* representative of the best teachers, and that a larger sampling of good teachers would have yielded the same variety of answers.

That means that, had this been a test, most of the country's top English teachers would have, as we used to say, *flunked*.

And if most of the *top* teachers would have failed, what percentage of *average or poor* English teachers would we expect to fail?

And if the great preponderance of them would fail, *what kind of grammatical skill might we expect of the students they teach?*

The important point of all this is:

If you fall short in your knowledge of grammar, syntax and other aspects of usage, *stop blaming yourself,* or blaming yourself alone. It's a shared responsibility. And, based on my unscientific sample, it seems likely that the odds were stacked against you from the start.

CHAPTER 3

Millstones of Usage

If languages were canine, English would be a mutt. Of very mixed parentage, it is a language whose parts collide as often as they blend.

Good writers came along 'way before grammarians did. Grammar is a somewhat recent arrival, a belated attempt to corral what seemed--at least to purists--an anarchic and seemingly insolent language. Once set into place, the structure of English grammar (or American grammar, to the extent that it differs) has grown rigid and unbending--a Semi-Immovable Object facing the Irresistible Force of our living language.

Every community still has outdated laws on its books that no one has bothered to erase. ("It is against the law in Pottsville to wear a red dress on Sunday.") These laws pose no problem; not even the most rock-jawed judge would dredge up and impose a law that dates back to bustles and buggywhips.

Grammar is like that. Times change; so does usage. Unfortunately, many grammarists do not, and continue to endorse and enforce "rules" that not only no longer make sense but, worse, maybe never did.

I've coined the word "grammarist" to differentiate it from "grammarian"--a student of and expert in grammar. The coined term includes others whose job, or whose inclination, it is to judge the correctness of others' language. Chief judges are teachers and bosses. These are the "grammarists" I mean.

Here are some millstones that manage to hang around, but really ought to be plopped in the millpond and let sink. *Whereas some "rules" are worth debating, these really are not. Forget them.*

Millstone 1. Don't start sentences with connective words--especially ***and, but,*** **and** ***however.***

Ignore this "rule," and drown in memory whoever laid it down for you.

The prohibition against *and* as a starter has been branded a "prejudice" by one grammarian and a "faintly lingering superstition" by H.W. Fowler, still the authority's authority on usage. And that was

60 years ago; the lingering ought to be very faint by now. But objectors continue to mutter as loudly as ever, even though writers as far back as the Bible have made good use of the starting *and*. (No, of course they didn't all write English.)

One caution, though, is not to strain so its use sounds phony, or overdo it, leading folks to suspect you're hard put for other ways to start. The worst aspect is the general, even bland, nature of the connection *and* provides--especially when more-specific linking words exist:

> It was a difficult year for "Suture Self" Home Surgical Kits. And the company did just fine.
> [*Try these instead:* but, nevertheless, yet, *or* in spite of that]

> Fewer students are interested in reading. And more educational money is going into video and software.
> [*Try these instead:* because of this, as a result, hence, *or* accordingly]

I suspect the anti-*and* "rule" often comes about through the grade-school teacher's desperate attempt to stop little kids from talking in a continuous sentence: "And then I went to the store and then Mommy bought me a grenadine popsicle and I saw a dog in the store and I tried to pat his head and said nice puppy and he bit me and so I cut him out of my will...."

"Yaaaaaa!" the teacher eventually screams, then tells the kid to stow all those *and*s, for Pete's sake, and start sentences without them. This expedient works, and soon grows into a "rule" that impairs the student for years.

Fewer people object to *but* as a starter. That's a good sign; it is a very useful sentence beginner, and completely okay.

Opponents of *however*--er, however--are deeply dug in. There is no reason at all behind their opposition. It happens to be an excellent transitional word. There is nothing wrong with it; still, you may have to fight in the trenches for its use.

The risks in employing *however* are three:

➡ That you will overuse it. There are equally good transitions meaning the same thing, like *nevertheless, in spite of that, yet,* and *still* (none of which, interestingly, seem to draw much criticism).

➡ That it will be placed wrongly. It ought to be spotted so as to throw contrast against what precedes it, as in:

The President was supposed to speak. <u>However</u>, he was bothered by laryngitis, so his speech was delivered by his wife.

Not:

The President was supposed to speak. He was bothered by laryngitis, so his speech was delivered by his wife, <u>however</u>.

• Most damaging, that *however* will be asked to do double duty:

The police force was at maximum readiness. The disturbances at Keeney Square Friday caught them off guard, <u>however</u>, they responded rapidly to the situation and had things under control within an hour.

Does the *however* intend to contrast the police's readiness with their being caught off guard? Or does it intend to contrast their being off guard with their ability to respond fast? Or does it seek to do both? In that case, two *howevers* are required or, better, a *however* and an equivalent word.

The police force was at maximum readiness. However, the disturbances at Keeney Square Friday caught them off guard. Nevertheless, they responded rapidly......

We'll deal further with the use and misuse of connectors later in this book. For now, just remember to dunk the millstone rule that has kept you from using these useful sentence starters.

Millstone 2. Don't split infinitives.

Although English descended from many language parents, the only one that had a formal grammar book was Latin. So the early grammarians used it as a model. But Latin ain't English, and an attempt to make it come close was about like cramming Cinderella's stepsisters' huge feet into Cindy's little shoes.

(There is also the common charge that snobbery played a big part in the choice of Latin. Only the intellectuals--spell that, wealthy-- knew Latin. So grammar books, far from being an attempt to help people use correct English, were in many cases status symbols meant to reinforce existing class distinctions.)

But we are stuck with it. Well, no, we really aren't. Not just excellent writers but also plain folks--either through ignorance, not caring or, often, common sense--have managed to use most of the helpful parts of grammar books and dispose of most of the stupid ones.

"If I read 'upcoming' in the Wall Street Journal once more, I'll be downcoming and someone will be outgoing."

--Barney Kilgore, then editor of WSJ

Most of them. But not all. Along with useful principles of language, a lot of arbitrary ones have been defended and imposed by teachers and grammar book publishers. The classic, and one of the most senseless, is the stricture against splitting the infinitive.

An infinitive is the form of any verb that begins with *to*, as in *to run, to eat, to snigger, to chortle, to ululate*.

In Latin you would have to take an axe to split an infinitive, since Latin infinitives are single words. Our infinitive *to hold* is *tenere* in Latin, for instance. Since Latin infinitives are unsplittable, English ones also should be, the rule-setters insisted.

That was how it began. However, teachers over the years have invented supplemental reasons not to split infinitives--enough reasons that the "rule" has persisted as one of the more scary "don't's" that paralyze people trying to write. A former Governor of Washington would rebuff and even demote staff assistants who submitted drafts to her with split infinitives in them.

Well, do any good reasons exist for not splitting infinitives?

I suppose there is a teensy risk that some nincompoop might jam half of his or her life history in between the *to* and the action word.

> I liked **to**, whenever time allowed it and I had no further duties to perform such as I typically was assigned by either my parents or my grandparents, **fish**.

Other than that, the English infinitive, with its little divider space, not only is easy to split but also often ought to be split.

What does this mean?

> They demanded promptly to be informed of any changes in position.

Did they demand promptly? Or did they wish to be promptly informed? This version--the natural way to put it--makes it clear:

> They demanded to be promptly informed of any changes in position.

In English, the normal place for an adverb is just before the verb it modifies. So infinitive-splitting falls right in line with the principle: Keep related parts together.

Millstone 3. Don't use sentence fragments.

Is it ever okay to use a sentence fragment? Yes. Expert writers

16

hundreds of years have done so--long before the rule was set down prohibiting it.

What is a "sentence fragment" anyway? Viewpoints vary, but all agree a fragment is something less than a full sentence. Given that, we can assume that it arises in one of three ways:

1. Through grammatical ignorance. Not knowing, for instance, that a sentence must have a subject and a verb:

> He brought someone else with him. *His brother Willie, from Umberton, North Carolina.*
>
> *One of the most important things I want to talk to you about.*

Or by not realizing that when you tack connectors onto that subject and verb, you must be sure they also connect to something else:

> [Because] he felt he was one of the better employees in the whole department, if not the whole company.

Such a careless or ignorant error is something an editor ought to correct. It isn't the most common kind of fragment, however.

2. Through deliberate choice--for emphasis, variety or compactness.

Here the fragment has proven useful for centuries. Check your favorite writer. If you find that he or she never uses fragments, I owe you a lunch. (This chapter has already used half a dozen.)

Here is a quick sampling of current authors:

> The object of storytelling is not to explain or resolve, but rather to create and to perform miracles of the imagination. *To extend the boundaries of the mysterious.* (Tim O'Brien.)
>
> My problem is that books don't get written that way. *Especially not books containing truth.* (Erica Jong.)
>
> How about "The earth is round?" *Strange territory, that one.* (T.R. Hummer.)
>
> What advice do you have for young writers? *Oh, the usual stuff about reading and about committing yourself to your work.* (Hilma Wolitzer.)

If we were restricted to nothing but complete sentences, writing

"Language, left alone, always tends to purify itself."

-- Philip Gore, editor, Webster's Third New Int'l Dictionary

would be radically changed. Writers have over the years developed a variety of shorthand techniques, of which the fragment is only one. The truth is, a good part of what we call sentences are incomplete. Some are pretty large fragments, others small ones.

Here are some medium-sized fragments:

> John Scott's greatest single positive attribute was physical strength. Sean Mooney's, a kind spirit. Sydney Rizotti's, an unending sense of humor.

The omitted words above total 10; twice, a comma replaces *greatest single positive attribute was.*

Here is a small fragment, with the omitted words added in brackets:

> Are we going to knuckle under to pressure from various fringe groups, and thereby abandon the principles that have brought us this far? Not on your life [are we going to knuckle under to pressure from various fringe groups and thereby abandon the principles that have brought us this far]!

As you may conclude, every simple "Yes" or "No" answer is a fragment; the rest of the sentence is implied by the question.

3. Through the influence of advertising.

Don't read this chapter as a license for willy-nilly slicing up sentences. Fragmentation can go too far. Where it most often does is in the work of ad copywriters.

Advertising has produced both creative geniuses and witless hacks--in nowhere near equal numbers. The geniuses typically progress to management, directing and ownership; the hacks keep hacking--pumping out thoughtless stuff like this over-chowdered piece of copy:

> The design staff at Ditmar's wants to help create a home that pleases you. One that reflects the best of you and your family. And stays within your budget. Together we will find the right elements. At the best values. For your home.

So, what are the guidelines for using sentence fragments?

➥ The main one is to use them in a way that shows you know you're doing it, that it's not a clumsy error. To do this, it usually helps not to begin a sentence as if it might finish, then stop short-- like this one (underlined):

19

> The company needs a tighter control of hiring certain categories. <u>Professional personnel and technical support, for instance.</u>

The reader, who might expect the second sentence to say: *Professional personnel and technical support, for instance, should be carefully selected* finds instead that you're already done.

By contrast, here you clearly signal a deliberate fragment:

> Subscription revenue is not meeting production costs. <u>Which is only one reason to increase our rates.</u>

➥ The second guideline is, don't overdo them. But don't skimp on them, either, if your style seems to call for them. For instance, here is an effective paragraph, but one that would cause the fussbudget editor to have apoplexy, since it is made up of nothing but fragments:

> So, what about the growing difference between the rich and poor? Put more specifically, the increasing gap between wealthy countries and impoverished ones. Any promises from any of the candidates? Probably not, other than passionate vows of commitment that, for the good of global society as a whole, the problem "must be solved." Easier said than done, of course: additional financial aid from the more fortunate countries, educational programs for the poor nations' infrastructures, increasing exchanges of technical personnel. Impressive sounding, well-meant and maybe even workable, but so far only words, not deeds.

➥ The third is, keep most of them short. A fairly common cause of fragments is that a sentence gets so long and complex that the writer loses track and simply inserts a period.

We'll end with this example--not the world record-holder, but long as "fragments" go:

> During the second year of the NCNB, which is a derivative of the MCCP and its philosophy, whereby neighborhood associations have an opportunity to promulgate their local issues from a much broader base, thereby creating the kind of unity that is so vitally needed in our family of nine neighborhoods, which comprises over 100,000 citizens.

So, just what was it that happened "during the second year of the NCNB?" Sadly, none of us will never know.

Millstone 4. Don't end a sentence with a preposition.

Here we arrive at probably the most common collision between the "don't's" of grammar and the "do's" of common sense. For every time that following the rule makes a clearer sentence, there will be a time or two when doing so makes a clumsy one.

Churchill may or may not have said of this rule:

> This is the sort of arrant pedantry [or arbitrariness, or damned nonsense] up with which I will not put.

Certainly he didn't say all three versions. But it makes a good story, and a good point: If you follow the rule slavishly, you may say something silly that you might have said clearly.

The key word is "may." If you use a Workaround, there often is a third way, one that abides by the rule and doesn't sound awkward.

> I will not put up with this sort of arrant pedantry.

But it is hard to see how these rule-breaking sentences could be said much more pointedly:

> These are the best fruits to make candy of.
> He ate every one he could get his hands on.
> This depends on whom they are paired with.
> What locker is your coat in?
> It's hard to know what he is really after.

And if the apparent "preposition" is really part of what's called a phrasal verb, in which the verb and adverb are seen as one unit (*give up, catch up, play down, knock out, look over*), there is no sensible way you can separate the two words.

> Here are the records over which you wanted to look.

That was the case, incidentally, with the Churchill remark above --so his example, even though making the point, was flawed. It will also be the case, I predict, with two-thirds of the ending "prepositions" your reviewer will pounce on. (Not, on which your reviewer will pounce.)

Sometimes, noted Theodore Bernstein, a terminal preposition can sound like the final puttputt of a dying engine:

> Of all the jerkwater towns in America, the sleepy little upper New York state burg of South Jackhammer was the one he least wanted to go to.

Your sentence should always end strongly. It's best to work around examples like that one.

But if your choice is to be correct or say something clearly, there is no choice. The no-ending-preposition rule was once, said H.W. Fowler, a "cherished superstition"--but one that most good writers snubbed. So it is hardly a rule anyway, despite the dogged efforts of grammarists who still find glee in red-penciling violations.

Millstone 5. A paragraph has to have at least two sentences.

Booshwah.

A writer trying to stick to that one could unnecessarily dilute her point. Famous one-sentence paragraphs would lose impact while they gain "correctness."

> I came, I saw, I conquered. And I also enjoyed the scenery.

> Ask not what your country can do for you; ask what you can do for your country. Or your city, or at least your local school district.

> War is hell. And South Dakota is no great shakes either.

> I know not what course others may take but, as for me, give me liberty or give me death! Or, as a third option, early retirement and a little home in the country.

Single-sentence paragraphs can emphasize an idea or provide a nice change of pace. Overused, they will do neither one. But you're unlikely to overuse them.

ADDENDUM: in Defense of Idiom

You might advise someone to "put your better foot forward," which is grammatically correct. But you would come off sounding like a prep-school snot.

If you were to note that your daughter fell "heels over head" in love, that would get you funny looks too--even though the idiomatic "head over heels" conveys no picture of tumbling at all. (Think about it for a minute.)

Idiom says "put your **best** foot forward," and not even a stickler for language would suggest this means you have three or more feet. But a lot of bosses red-pencil equally idiomatic expressions.

What is idiom? It is usage whose common meaning differs from its literal one. Most idiom has lasted long enough to be accepted, whether or not it is "right." Some picky reviewers feel superior to idiomatic language, and hack it out when they spot it. This section

"The fact is that the remarkable freedom enjoyed by English in putting its prepositions late...is an important element in the flexibility of the language."

--H.W. Fowler

may help in your defense should you need to confront such a hacker.

Climb Down

Yes, when we say *climb* we do usually mean ascent. But no, there is nothing disreputable about *climb down*. In such a sentence as *The delegate was forced to climb down from his lofty moral position,* the phrase *climb down* suggests a more active and reluctant effort than *descend* or *come down*. (The reviewer who balks at *climb down* will also nail you when you write that a plane lands on water. A plane can't *land* on water, he will say, poking your rib on the word *land*. Perhaps he's right. Luckily, seaplane pilots don't know that.)

Can't Seem

Yes, *We can't seem to get the details worked out* is grammatically incorrect. No, it would not necessarily be better to say *We seem unable to get the details worked out.* Idiomatically the first version is probably the stronger. At any rate, it is very well accepted.

Everybody Else's

Everybody's else job has been upgraded. That is linguistically correct. But if your editor tries to force such a stilted usage on you, he or she has a tin ear, tinnier than--well, everybody else's.

I Don't Think

You write, *I don't think the plant windows are water-tight.*

But you do think, chides the editor, knowing everything; so the sentence is wrong. No, the editor is wrong. Here the modifier *not* (in *don't*) is what is called a sentence adverb, modifying the entire statement, not just the verb *think.* Similarly, *I never burped in church* doesn't mean you never burped.

This editor, I bet, will also note that to *send no money* is impossible. What would you put no money in, for instance? he may inquire. Give him this test: Have him ask 100 people to send him no money. He'll get 100 per cent response.

In Half

The stickler will point out correctly that you cut a budget *in halves,* not in *half.* But the idiomatic *in half* dates back to Dickens. Would this fusser also bristle at other idiomatic uses of *half? Half an hour* (never *quarter an hour*), *not half bad* (never *not third bad*)?

Men Employees, Women Employees

The editor may argue that, since most plural nouns take singular possessives (*child prodigies, grownup patients, boy sopranos, girl athletes*), the correct wording should be *man employees* and *woman employees*. But idiom is idiom. Use the plural *men* and *women*, and the singular in all other instances. Otherwise you will sound odd and your friends will look at you funny.

CHAPTER 4

Greasing the Skids

Writing more correctly has more to it than improving your grammar. You can take several steps right now to decrease the likelihood of errors. None of them require you to learn anything new. Together, they will grease the skids to make your writing improvement a far smoother process.

1.Write more concisely.

Concise writing and correct writing relate. It is easier, however, to see the link between wordiness and structural mistakes.

Of the two partners in verbosity--long words and long sentences --the latter is the more likely to cause usage errors. Language problems become far more common, and severe, when sentences begin to get long and to ramble.

Two good examples--among the writers' most common problems--are subject-verb disagreements and unattached modifying phrases, especially the notorious "dangling participle." Both increase with sentence length.

∞ **Subject-verb squabbles**

No one would write:

> Bill Clinton are our president.

But someone wrote this:

> The major **cause** of many, perhaps all, of our current society's major social and political problems **are** found in poverty and malnutrition.

The cause of that problem are found in sentence length plus writer carelessness.

You'll have little trouble keeping subject and verb together if your sentence is short; in fact, in a short sentence, subject and verb can't really **get** very far apart. But in a longer sentence, other nouns may intrude and distract the writer. In the above example, the adjoining words *problems are* looked right to their author, who then probably didn't re-read the final product.

Try to keep your eye on the subject in this lengthy sentence portion:

> The first one of the new glass-and-steel structures to be constructed by the new company near the junction of our two major highways are nearing completion.

You probably managed to keep track of it. But the writer didn't-- possibly distracted by the words *highways are* or perhaps *structures....are*. The correct subject and verb are **one...is.**

⇨ Dangling participles and their kin

A raincloud moving with the wind will dump its load of water on the first mountain peak it comes to. In the same way, a group of words that starts a sentence and has no subject of its own will tend to find one by hooking onto the first thing that follows, creating silliness like this:

> Sitting on the hood of my car, I saw a yellow-bellied sapsucker.

> After reading several biographies of him, Hitler seems to have been truly both a madman and a genius.

The second example is a classic dangling participle (see page 94), in that the real subject isn't even mentioned--the person (*I*) who had read the biographies. But most orphan phrases don't really "dangle" very long; instead, they adopt the first likely noun that comes along.

Participles aren't the only culprits. Here are some other misplaced phrases:

> On third base and spitting tobacco juice, Mrs. Jones thought Kelly looked like a nicotine-stained Greek god, not a baseball player.

> Comfortable and cool inside the fish tank, the cat could see three piranhas taunting him with Jimmy Cagney imitations.

> Although fat and greasy and smelling of onions, Dooley wolfed down the hamburger.

Clauses cause fewer problems than phrases because clauses contain subjects as well as verbs. But clauses can dangle also, especially if they contain personal pronouns:

> Even though he could "sit" and "roll over" on command, Studs Jensen considered his dog stupid.

26

This version would have been clear:

> Even though his dog could "sit" and "roll over" on command, Studs Jensen considered him stupid.

How does conciseness work against danglers? In a very direct way: If you write mostly with single-thought sentences, there will be fewer lead-in phrases and clauses of any kind, including dangling ones.

2.Re-read your own material carefully.

This may seem to be an obvious and unneeded piece of advice. Obvious, maybe. Unneeded, no. The single most predictable problem with anyone's writing is that it will be filled with *inconsistencies--* inconsistencies that a good re-reading would have caught.

Look carefully at this example:

> Management of Father Knows Wurst Sausage Co. believes that the Company's financial condition positions it well for the future. Working capital of the company has varied between thirty per cent of net sales and 45 per cent for the last three years. A substantial portion of assets is represented by short-term investments overseas. Maturing long term debt increased in 1990, but decreased in 1991, when The Company's $35 million principal amount of 8-year notes matured.

An okay piece of writing. No grammar or syntax errors. But look at the inconsistent use of capitalization: Is it to be *the Company* (line 2), *the company* (line 3) or *The Company* (line 7)?

Similarly, the *thirty per cent* on line 4 ought to be followed by *forty-five per cent* rather than *45 per cent*. Or else--and this is preferable--both should be numbers: *30* and *45*. There is a similar inconsistency between *three years* and *8-year notes*. And between *short-term investments* (hyphenated) and *long term debt* (not hyphenated).

Two points in this regard:

∞ Even a non-expert in grammar can notice these discrepancies. If you write *dinosour* on one line and *dinnasaur* on the next, even a dullard who doesn't know how to spell it himself will reckon you got it wrong at least once.

∞ A related point: You don't have to learn any more grammar than you already know to re-read for consistency.

"When unsure [about how to word a sentence] the simplest way out, as always, is to seek some other method of expressing the thought...There is no more hazardous mental occupation [than lapsing] into a profound study of a grammatical situation."

--James Thurber

Why do people often not carefully re-read their writing? Here are some possible reasons:

1. They count on someone else to do it. That "someone else" may be spellchecker or grammarchecker software--which has only limited capability.

2. They don't allow enough time in their writing schedule for a thoughtful re-reading.

3. They just can't stand to look at the fool thing one more time.

Here are some suggestions that may help you re-read:

∽ If you revise while you write, be sure to read each edited sentence in its entirety before you move on. A common habit is to read just far enough back to get a good running start. For instance, in this non-sensible example:

> The reason for the increasing rate of reported cracks in nuclear-plant equipment is caused by better record-keeping, not poorer construction.

The nonsense sentence, *The reason....is caused by better record-keeping, etc.* possibly arose because the writer, trying to decide between *better record-keeping rather than poorer construction* and *better record-keeping, not poorer construction,* read back only as far as:

> ...the increasing rate of reported cracks in nuclear-plant equipment...

and finished it:

> ...the increasing rate of reported cracks in nuclear-plant equipment is caused by better record-keeping, not poorer construction.

That sounds all right. However, the complete sentence now reads, incorrectly:

> The **reason** for the increasing rate of reported cracks in nuclear-plant equipment **is caused** by better record-keeping, not poorer construction.

The following mishmash also may have been caused by failing to re-read the full sentence. (Slash mark/ indicates the point where the re-reading probably began:)

> Management of the company attributes/ this change in trend of order volume **resulted** from an improved economic environment.

"It is quite impossible to stop the progress of language. Words and expressions will be forced into use in spite of all the exertions of all the writers in the world."
--Noah Webster

So, re-read each sentence fully as you revise. If you're editing someone else's writing, pay particular attention to doing this.

∾ Adjust your schedule to allow ample time between the draft and the final re-reading. If you read while the words are hot off the brain, they will say just about what you expect them to say. A day later--all right, a couple of hours later--inconsistencies and other slips are more likely to show up.

3. Do a bit of non-job reading each day.

Not only will a daily ration of reading good writing provide an antidote to the wordy, poorly organized and otherwise flawed job-related documents that cross your desk; it also will give you a chance to observe the application by good writers of the principles discussed in this book.

Try to use, as case studies, serious writing done by recognized good writers; secondly, things that are likely to have been carefully edited. Books are better in this respect than magazines; magazines better than daily newspapers, where the speed of production often reduces the attention given to editing. Avoid the work of humor writers, who often gain some of their comic effect by clowning with language, including deliberate grammar-mauling.

You don't need to read a lot; a couple of pages daily--thought-fully perused--will be adequate. As you read, look at how the writer uses words, sentence structure, clauses, verbs; how well he or she practices what this book preaches.

4. Learn to do workarounds.

This is the biggest favor you can do yourself. Suppose you find yourself in mid-sentence, and stuck. You can't figure out whether to say:

> He is the person **whom** you said was the best lawyer in Seattle.

or

> He is the person **who** you said was the best lawyer in Seattle.

And both ways look right, or neither does. Don't get into a snit over it and stare at it until your train of thought is broken. There are always other ways to make a point; select one of those instead. House carpenters have a nice term for it when a planned approach to building fails. They call it "workarounds"--working around the problem area rather than being immobilized by it.

Instead of the example above, either of these versions would work:

> He is the best lawyer in Seattle, you said.
> He is the person you said is the best lawyer in Seattle.

And, just so you don't feel you're ducking the problem, jot down the offending sentence and solve it later. Just don't let it stall your writing flow.

5. Develop a set of agreed-on writing standards.

The truth is, a lot of grammatical and syntactical issues are matters of preference rather than of absolute right or wrong. (Not every editor will admit it; but it's true.)

But, whether they reflect editorial preference or true correctness, disagreements with the boss over writing matters are no fun. Best to avoid them. Developing a set of standards that you both can agree on is the best way to reduce the number of head-buttings the two of you will have to do.

How to produce a useful set of standards:

∞ An easy way is to buy a reputable style guide--and, if needed, modify it to fit boss's or editor's preference, or company or agency style requirements. Thoughtful style books by The New York Times, The Chicago Tribune, The Associated Press and The Washington Post are available at bookstores. They all mix an understanding of correctness with a common-sense appreciation of clear writing. To varying degrees, each gives reasons for its recommendations. They are not merely unreasoning "rulebooks."

Some organizations use the US Government Style Manual, which, in addition to being gosh-awfully long, does little in the way of explaining the rationale for its choices. It is arbitrary, somewhat military in tone and not very interesting reading.

In choosing a style guide, here are two approaches:

1. Ask your reviewer which manual he or she recommends. Odds are, you'll get a blank stare. But perhaps not; he or she may come up with a name. Otherwise, you choose.

Author H. L. Mencken was never known to mince words. Here are some unminced ones:

"With precious few exceptions, all the books on style in English are by writers quite unable to write. The subject, indeed, seems to exercise a special and dreadful fascination over school ma'ams, bucolic college professors, and other such pseudo-literates...Their central aim, of course, is to reduce the whole thing to a series of simple rules--the overmastering passion of their melancholy order, at all times and everywhere."

31

2. If you're free to make the choice, might as well pick one whose preferences agree with your own, on such things as capitalization, commas before *and*, number style and so on.

☞ Or you can create your own customized standards guidebook, based on editorial corrections you get from your boss. This may be the most useful way to go, for two reasons:

➼ The guidebook will be short and manageable, limited to those style issues that cause problems or are unique to your company or your situation.

➼ The reviewer will have played a role in its creation; it is a collaborative effort.

To build such a stylebook, here is the way to proceed:

Each time you receive a specific correction, try to find the principle behind it. For instance, if the editor changes your words *Field Engineer* to *field engineer*, ask whether that means job titles are never to be capitalized. It may be, instead, that company policy is to capitalize the term if it precedes someone's name (*Field Engineer Wendy Cliff*) but not when it follows the name (*Wendy Cliff, field engineer*).

Make sure your editor verifies each entry in your stylebook, to avoid misunderstandings.

There is a lot of value to having a written set of standards. The main one, of course, is that it reduces the number of corrections, thus saving both your time and the editor's. And your eagerness to compile it shows an interest in better writing, an enthusiasm that your reviewer can't help but notice.

Straightforward Writing:
The Five Principles

CHAPTER 5

How Language Works

I. SHORTCUTS

(A disclaimer: This bit of English history is not accurate. But lurking in the whimsy is an important point about the unending battle between grammar and actual usage:)

No sooner had the Laws of Grammar been enacted than folks began violating them. Among the earliest violators were poets, who couldn't make things rhyme without fiddling around with language in grammatically illegal ways. For instance,

> When ye olde man's feeling goode
> He woode like to watch TV

didn't rhyme. So the poet would scramble up the words a bit:

> When ye olde man's feeling goode
> Like to watch TV he woode
> And he'd settle in ye chair
> Whenever he would get ye urge....Oops!

Rearranging the the word order helped--but not enough:

> He would get ye urge whenever

So, unable to think of another word to rhyme with *chair*, he simply removed the letter *v* from *whenever*.

> And he'd settle in his chair
> He would get ye urge whene'er

They did the same thing with *even* and *over*, changing them to *e'en* and *o'er*, thereby gaining rhymes for *smithereen* and *thermidor*, two of their favorite subjects.

It is a little-known fact that many of today's greatest poems were written by poets with a price on their heads for breaking grammar laws. Shakespeare himself was tormented by grammar. His greatest soliloquy dealt with which intransitive verb was correct: "'To be' or not 'to be'?" he kept asking his wife, a former English teacher, who eventually divorced him, claiming incompatibility and endless pestering.

Grammarians, sore as anything about poets' ignoring the rules, asked the government to tax them. The King responded by forcing every rhyme-maker to buy a Poetic License (the cost varying with the weight of the poem). So that solved that.

However, pretty soon English peasants and other illiterate folks unable to read the Rules of Grammar also began to take shortcuts in usage. Fearing that if the government clamped down, the people would revolt and storm the Bastille (which, as a precaution, had been located in France), grammarians decided just to let it ride.

The true point in this false history is that everyday usage over the centuries has knocked the corners off textbook English. For efficiency or just ease of use, talkers and writers have streamlined the language in three ways you need always to be aware of:

✳ They sometimes invert the standard subject-verb word order:

> INVERTED: This book, in which are found many examples of
> good advice, is available at all bookstores.
> STANDARD ORDER: This book, many <u>examples</u> of good advice <u>are</u>
> <u>found</u> in which...   SUBJECT   VERB

> INVERTED: The senator, whose endorsement both candidates sought,
> was hard to pin down.
> S.O.: The senator, both <u>candidates</u> <u>sought</u> whose <u>endorsement</u>....
>   SUBJECT   VERB   OBJECT

> INVERTED: Dog food he hates. Twinkies he eats!
> S.O.: <u>He</u> <u>hates</u> <u>dog food</u>. <u>He</u> <u>eats</u> <u>Twinkies!</u>
>   SUBJECT VERB OBJECT   SUBJECT VERB OBJECT

✳ They often leave understood words out:

> I know you feel we can react if we want.
> FULL SENTENCE: I know [that] you feel [that] we can react if we
> want [to react].
> Mildred likes Joanie better than [she likes] John.
> It is not true that pasta makes you fat; if it were [true that pasta
> makes you fat], I wouldn't touch it.
> The company gave [to] John a trophy. (*This one also slightly inverts the
> standard order; that would be:* The company gave a trophy to John.)

✳ They pinch-hit with pronouns. This shorthand characteristic is built into grammar itself. If it were not for the pronouns *their, them, he,* and *his,* we would have to write:

> Although Shakespeare's audiences were illiterate, Shakespeare
> was popular with Shakespeare's audiences because Shakespeare's

36

audiences felt that Shakespeare spoke the language of Shakespeare's audiences.

Although <u>his</u> audiences were illiterate, Shakespeare was popular with <u>them</u> because <u>they</u> felt <u>he</u> spoke <u>their</u> language.

If it were not for the pronoun *which*, we would have to write:

My hunting jacket, the garment you admired this morning, is hand-made.

My hunting jacket, <u>which</u> you admired this morning, is hand-made.

Keeping these streamlining features in mind will make the

job of analyzing sentences easier. Structural principles of language work pretty well, but they are based on standard word order with no omitted words.

For instance:

In the book he borrowed was found a folded note.

You'll make the sentence far easier to analyze if you first re-insert omitted words, put all parts into standard order and, when possible, replace pronouns with the nouns they represent:

1. Insert the omitted word *that*.

In the book **that** he borrowed was found a folded note.

2. Substitute the noun *the book* for its pronoun *that*.

~~that~~
/ **the book** he borrowed/

In the book/   /was found a folded note.

3. Finally, put all words into standard subject/verb order. Now it is a simple matter to spot the two clauses and the true subjects and verbs of each:

~~that~~
he <u>borrowed</u> the book

SUBJECT   VERB   OBJECT

A folded <u>note</u> <u>was found</u> in the book

SUBJECT   VERB

In later chapters, when we discuss phrases, clauses and sentences, this preliminary procedure will come in very handy. We'll refer to it as Clearing the Deck.

II. PARTS AND SUBASSEMBLIES

The average person, estimating how many parts of speech there are, might guess anywhere from dozens to maybe hundreds.

That's probably because of the log-jam of grammar terms clogging his mind: noun, subjunctive, voice, tense, verb, clause, participle, predicate, genitive, objective, preposition, case, imperative, absolute, interrogative, pronoun, metaphor, mood...It is too much; they get all mixed up.

There are only eight parts of speech--and only seven that matter. These parts fall into five categories:

❋ Solids--Their **names: nouns and pronouns

❋ Movers--Their **name:** verbs

❋ Describers--Their **names:** adverbs and adjectives

❋ Connectors--Their **names**: conjunctions and prepositions

❋ Interjections (unimportant)

Each word has, besides a name, a **job** to do in a sentence. There are six distinct jobs:

❋ Subject

❋ Verb

❋ Completer

❋ Modifier

❋ Link

❋ Interrupter (unimportant)

To recap, each word has both a **name** (part of speech) and a **job** (function in a sentence). It's not difficult to keep these concepts separate--and very important that you do so.

A sentence may be analyzed at two levels: The **word** level and the **subassembly** level. Most confusion occurs at the subassembly level.

You might compare a sentence to a house. A house is made of 2x4s, nails, screws, plywood, glue, and other materials. That's one way to view it. Another is that a house is made of walls, floors, ceil-

"The more we know about language, the less we seem to feel sure about it. This is completely natural and healthy. Trepidation heightens our critical powers and makes us more receptive to suggestion. How do we get [a knack for recognizing what makes language fresh and interesting]? Write a lot. Read even more. And duck anyone who uses *dialectic* in a conversation."

--Carol Richardson

ings, stairs, roof, etc. And the walls, floors, etc. themselves are made of 2x4s, nails, screws, and the like.

With a few exceptions, individual words can't build sentences. They need to be combined into subassemblies--called clauses and phrases.

Clauses and phrases do the same six jobs in a sentence that a word does--and have mostly the same names.

As an example, the noun's job may be done by a word, a phrase or a clause.

NOUN USED AS OBJECT OF VERB

The policeman showed | his badge. *(noun phrase)*
bravery. *(single-word noun)*
symptoms of fatigue. *(noun phrase)*
that he could take a lot of ribbing from kids. *(noun clause)*

An adverb also may be a word, phrase or clause.

Cheerfully *(single-word adverb)*
Moving across the field *(adverb phrase)* | he whistled a tune.
As he moved across the field *(adverb clause)*

So may an adjective:

The old car was rusty. *(single-word adjective)*
The car that was left in the car wash over Christmas made the headlines. *(adjective clause)*
The car referred to in the paper is the same one we're talking about. *(adjective phrase)*

The point of this book is to help you write living sentences, not do post mortems on dead ones. But it's useful at this point to look at just one sentence at both its word level and its various assembly levels. Like all the page examples in this book, it is worth studying-- and then referring to again after you read successive chapters.

The example is on the next page:

"What may be legitimately resisted are, first, the assumption that if a thousand illiterates utter a certain locution over a period of two years that locution becomes a rule of English and, second, the presumption of grammatical authoritarians that they can draw on prejudices or illogical fantasies to lay down arbitrary rules."

--Theodore Bernstein

THE SENTENCE: The convict ate nine boxes of chocolate because he had heard that he would be sure to break out.

At the **word** level, here are some combinations:

The (*adjective*) convict (*noun*) NOUN PHRASE

nine (*adjective*) boxes (*noun*) NOUN PHRASE

of (*preposition*) chocolate (*noun*) PREPOSITIONAL PHRASE

he (*pronoun*) had heard (*verb*) CLAUSE

he (*pronoun*) would be (*verb*) sure (*adjective*) CLAUSE

to break (*infinitive*) out (*adverb*) INFINITIVE☛ PHRASE

At the **subassembly** level, combining the above words, phrases and clauses:

nine boxes / of chocolate NOUN PHRASE CONTAINING PREPOSITIONAL PHRASE

The convict / ate (*verb*) / nine boxes of chocolate CLAUSE CONTAINING NOUN PHRASE

that he would be sure / to break out DEPENDENT CLAUSE CONTAINING INFINITIVE☛ PHRASE

he had heard / that he would be sure to break out INDEPENDENT CLAUSE CONTAINING DEPENDENT CLAUSE

Assembling the pieces, and adding *because* and *that*, we see the whole sentence:

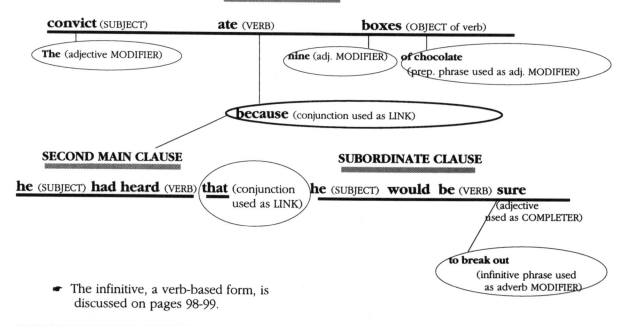

☛ The infinitive, a verb-based form, is discussed on pages 98-99.

CHAPTER 6

Sharpening your Clause

Whoever said everything is a story hit on something.

Any piece of writing that works has a beginning and an end. And the reader must progress from start to finish as easily as she can. Some documents are truly narrative tales. Some are logical arguments; some, persuasive proposals; others, historical summaries; still others, technical analyses. Whatever it is, the message that fails to carry the reader from beginning to end on a straightforward path will stand little chance of being effective.

The message must move the reader forward. The key to writing that does so--Straightforward Writing--is the clause. It is the critical building block of language.

Why is the clause vital?

•• The clause is the only element that by itself can carry a complete thought. Individual words can't do it.✏ Phrases can't do it. Words and phrases combined by the dozens can't do it. **To express a complete thought, you need a clause.**

•• The clause carries **all** the direct movement of your writing. Everything else to some extent rides along with it.

•• The clause contains **more information** than any other sentence element.

What is a clause?

It is a related group of words that

1. Contains both a subject and a verb, and

2. Can either

   * Stand alone and convey an idea, or

   * Serve as some part of speech--noun, pronoun, adverb, adjective.

Information in a sentence should answer three questions. (It must

"Everything which is written is meant either to please or to instruct. This second object is difficult to effect without attending to the first."

--Sidney Smith

☛Except for single-word commands, in which the subject "You" is clearly implied.

answer two, and it may also answer others.) The three that should be answered are:

❋ Who or **what** is

- ↪ Doing whatever is being done. (*He will order pizza.*)
- ↪ Possessing whatever is being possessed. (*She has a cold.*)
- ↪ Existing in a certain condition. (*They were drowsy.*)

❋ Whether that thing or person

- ↪ Is doing something. (*He **will order** pizza.*)
- ↪ Is possessing something. (*She **has** a cold.*)
- ↪ Is existing in a certain condition. (*They **were** drowsy.*)

❋ And just **when** this happens.

- ↪ *He **will order** pizza.* (Sometime in the future.)
- ↪ *She **has** a cold.* (Right now.)
- ↪ *They **were** drowsy.* (They no longer are.)

An active-verb clause (the subject performs the action) tells you all three of these things. It is the only unit of language that is able to do that.

It also commonly answers a fourth question:

❋ Who or **what** is

- ↪ Receiving the action. (*He will order **pizza.***) or
- ↪ Being possessed. (*She has a **cold.***)
  or

❋ Who, what or **what condition** is completing the action.
   (*They were **drowsy**.*)

It may also, as a bonus, tell you where, why and how, as this short clause does:

> The inhabitants there unsuccessfully hunt gooney birds for profit, using leaky traps.

In most grammar courses, clauses and phrases tend to be talked about in the same breath. But they shouldn't be. They differ in essential ways.

A (phrase) (to be discussed in chapter 10) is a related group of words that--unlike a clause--lacks subject or verb, or both. It has no way of conveying a complete thought. It can tell you who/what is the subject, or else what is/was/will be done, or when. But never all three, and seldom two.

>   Running down the long, red-carpeted staircase...

tells you the action but not the runner (who) or the time (when). Even in combination, phrases still fall short as information-packers:

>   Back in the olden days, the days of knighthood and fair maidens.....

The phrases there tell you when, but give no hint of action or who might have done that action.

>   A tall man with a white beard and a casual manner, slim as a popsicle and smiling at the crowd.....

Five phrases combined there, telling us who--but that's it. What is the man going to do, or what did he do, or what is he doing?

Not only does a clause give you answers to the key questions; it also generally keeps that information close together (unless you get cute with additional words, interruptive phrases and other kips and didoes). The clause thus follows a basic guide for Straightforward Writing: **Keep related ideas together.**

A useful concept when judging a sentence's effectiveness is that of **required memory span**--how far must a reader read before she can answer the key questions? It shouldn't be very far.

Here is a clause-driven version of a sentence. It gets to the point fast.

>   The large emerging pen-computer market will strengthen our 1994 profitability.

A phrase-based approach often takes its time:

>   Because of the large size of the emerging pen-computer market...

What's done? Who or what does it? When? Who knows? We must keep reading:

>   Because of the large size of the emerging pen-computer market, the effect on our 1994 profitability....

Effect will be--will be--what?

>   ...will be beneficial.
>   (*Complete sentence*) Because of the large size of the emerging pen-computer market, the effect on our 1994 profitability will be beneficial.

"Without question [the taboo] exists," noted Theodore Bernstein--"the taboo against starting a message with 'a','an' or 'the.'"

Writers over-conscious of this ruling often go to some other extreme.   Rather than, "The safety committee disapproved of new sewers in a strongly worded protest about the wording of the regulation." we often get a participial opening--with the ever-present possibility of the participle dangling:

"Strongly protesting the wording of the regulation, new sewers were... "

A reader would need some time to get to the point. Another fast-reading clause-driven version would have been:

> We expect profits will increase in 1994 because of the large emerging pen-computer market.

To take full advantage of clause power, you need to use a bit of discipline. That is, make sure that what **really is happening** is conveyed by the clause's subject and verb. Don't waste those words on abstractions or vague ideas. (Subjects and verbs underlined.)

> *(Two clauses; slow reading:)* Corrado's <u>argument</u> that Mrs. Wallis's <u>failure</u> to provide for preservation of wetland buffer zones upon expiration of the contract <u>discouraged</u> citizen-group challenges to that contract <u>has</u> no application here.

> *(Four clauses, fast reading:)* <u>Corrado argues</u> that when <u>Mrs. Wallis gave</u> no way to preserve the wetland buffer zones when t<u>he contract expired</u>, <u>she discouraged</u> citizen groups from challenging the contract. But that <u>argument does</u> not <u>apply</u> here.

Notice also that the subjects and verbs fit snugly together in the clause-heavy version. In the other sentence, similar in length, the subjects and verbs scatter.

On pages 51-52 you'll see several examples of both clause-shy and clause-driven writing. I recommend that you study them very carefully, to get a feeling for the contrast between each set of two examples. As you continue, bear in mind our first principle of Straightforward Writing:

> **1. STRAIGHTFORWARD WRITING IS DRIVEN BY CLAUSES.**

Grammarians, for all their precision, sometimes go along with some pretty loose definitions.

A clause, as we said, must have both a subject and a verb:

> The crowd roared.

And it remains technically a clause no matter how many words it adds, or how many phrases or even other clauses it absorbs. It still meets the definition: a related group of words with a subject and verb, that can stand alone or act as a part of speech. Here we have the same clause in a somewhat extended form:

> **The crowd** at the opening of the new arena **roared** to greet the entry into the ring of the champ, pug-nosed and squinty-eyed under the bright klieglights.

44

IT'S ALWAYS BEST not to say things you don't mean. People might think you do.

So it is useful to see the clause as made of its core (subject and verb) plus whatever additional language it accumulates. All that language will in the end either modify or tell about the subject, or modify or tell about the verb.

If a clause can stand alone, it is called an independent clause. If it does stand alone, it is called--a **sentence**. The simplest sentence you can write is a single independent clause. Write lots of them.

> The quick brown fox jumped over the lazy dog.
> Jesus wept.
> Einstein's reluctance to contribute to war weapons delayed the
> completion of his report to Roosevelt.

The more you can package your major ideas in independent clauses, the more straightforward your writing will be.

If the clause can't stand alone, keeps the reader on the edge of his seat, it is called a dependent clause. That doesn't mean it contains less information, only that it leaves a loose end. In fact, the way to convert an independent clause into a dependent one is to add to it:

> The engineers refused to move into the radiation area.
> (*Independent clause, stands alone and makes sense.*)
> **Because** the engineers refused to move into the radiation area....
> (*Dependent clause, now needing other information to complete
> the idea.*)

A dependent clause always serves as a single part of speech (its **name**) and plays a single role in a sentence (its **job**).

That part of speech may be a noun, just as it may with a single word. (Subject and verb of each dependent clause underlined):

> I know   wines.
> I know   that <u>he plays</u> tic-tac-toe for money.

It may be a pronoun, as a single word may:

> I'll give it to   him.
> I'll give it to   <u>whoever gets</u> here first.

It may be an adverb, modifying a verb:

> The elephant sneezed   loudly.
> The elephant sneezed   although <u>it took</u> several seconds from
>   start to finish.

"I could hardly write a sentence without dividing it down the middle with a semicolon. But my boss cured me. One day he strode into my office with a steel file and filed away the face of the semicolon key on my typewriter."

--Neil Morgan

46

It may be an adjective, modifying a noun or pronoun:

| The dachshund, | dog-tired, | fell into a deep sleep. |
| The dachshund, | who had lost his dog tag, | fell into a deep sleep. |

The simplest, and most common, sentence consists of one independent clause. Such sentences are your friends. Use them liberally.

But sentences often add to this main clause one or more dependent clauses. Many teachers encourage students to wallow in them. Most writers on style say use them sparingly. Straightforward Writing says they both miss the point.

You'll also find it useful now and then to have two or even more main clauses in one sentence.

And sometimes (seldom, if you are wise) your sentence will have multiple main clauses plus dependent ones.

(I'll elaborate fully on the above paragraphs in Chapter 11, Straightforward Sentences.)

The first step in understanding clauses is an easy one. Each clause, whatever its length, breaks down into two pieces: (1) Its complete subject and (2) its complete predicate, which is the verb and all attached words. (Don't bother remembering the word *predicate*, we won't use it after this chapter.)

At this level it's generally easy for you to tell where the break point is.☛

> **GRAMMATICALLY SPEAKING**
>
> If a sentence is a single independent clause it's called a **simple** sentence (no matter how difficult it gets). If it combines two or more independent clauses, it is called a **compound** sentence --and is in fact two simple sentences combined. If it has an independent clause and one or more dependent ones, it is a **complex** sentence. If you mix a compound and a complex sentence, you get--surprise!--a **compound-complex** sentence.
>
> None of this information is likely to help you write a bit better.

COMPLETE SUBJECT
The shy biology professor /

COMPLETE PREDICATE
/ blushingly described the reproduction process of the amoeba.

☛ Most grammar books oversimplify this by always using tidy sentences (as I have also), where everything before the breakpoint is the subject and everything after it is the predicate. But sometimes a predicate precedes or interrupts the subject, so don't be thrown if that happens. Note that these three sentences are identical except for word order:

1. The financial people used some "creative accounting" in figuring the year's profits.
2. In figuring the year's profits, the financial people used some "creative accounting."
3. The financial people, in figuring the year's profits, used some "creative accounting."

COMPLETE SUBJECT
How to reprimand without punishing/
COMPLETE PREDICATE
/must be learned by any good supervisor.

The next step can a little bit tougher--but it is important: that is to pull out from each of these two sections the key word or words in the subject (they are the **simple subject**) and the key word or words in the predicate (they are the **simple predicate.**)

The latter is the easy part: The heart of the predicate is always the verb itself.   Always.

SIMPLE PREDICATE
/ blushingly <u>described</u> the reproduction process of the amoeba.

Picking the simple subject is easy also--usually:

SIMPLE SUBJECT
The shy biology <u>professor/</u>

However, sometimes the simple subject is not a single word but several words. If no one of them can stand alone, the whole group becomes the simple subject.

SIMPLE SUBJECT
<u>How to reprimand without punishing/</u>

SIMPLE PREDICATE
/<u>must be learned</u> by any good supervisor.

The most common trouble occurs when the grammatical subject doesn't jibe with what your gut tells you is the real subject.

All of the beautiful diamonds shone in the sunlight.

In real life, almost anyone would see *diamonds* as the subject of the sentence. It fits the grammatical definition: The thing that is being spoken of. But, no: Grammar requires that *all* be the subject.

In the above sentence, figuring *diamonds* to be the subject would do no real harm; the sentence still reads correctly. But in the next sentence, wrongly identifying *children* as the subject causes a verb error:

Each of the children sing very well. (**Each**...**sings** very well.)

As you can see, the simple subject determines whether the verb is singular or plural. So you need to be good at picking it out.

Three tips may help you:

   The first noun or pronoun in the clause is usually its subject.

"Use familiar words. Be precise, but first be understood. Search for the solid nouns that bear the weight of thought. Use active verbs that hit an object and do not glance off."

48

THIS HALF-TIME TV INTERVIEW brought all-time low viewer ratings. Next time they'll choose an athlete who, y'know? talks like an athlete.

∽ The object of the preposition *of* (that is, the noun or pronoun following it) is never the subject of the clause containing that preposition.

∽ A general guide: Stay alert. The real subject and the grammatical subject sometimes differ, as we've seen.

Some things matter, some don't. **Nailing down the simple subject matters,** because it controls the verb and determines whether that verb is singular or plural.

This one stumbler is a main cause of subject-verb disagreements, and SVD's are perhaps the most common single grammar problem. So, before you continue, take a minute to locate the simple subjects in the next sentences, then choose the right verbs. Use the guidelines above if they'll help.

> One of the children is? are? snapping bubble gum in the
> balcony.
> (*Two clauses here*) I am surprised that each of the competitors
> has? have? a slight limp.
> (*Solve this complex sentence, and you get a gold star:*)
> The only one of those guys who ever say? says? "thank you" is
> Bluto--and he only mumbles.☛

The heart of every clause is its noun or pronoun **subject** and its **verb**. To produce Straightforward Writing, you need to become surefooted with these basic elements.

The next chapters will help you.

So will the full pages of examples placed throughout the book, comparing Straightforward Writing with less-readable styles. *These pages are pehaps the most useful portion of this book,* in that they directly convey the power and impact of the principles we discuss. I recommend that you study each such page (page 53 is the first such page), then review it after every major chapter.

☛ Answers:
> **One** of the children **is** snapping bubble gum in the balcony.
> I am surprised that **each** of the competitors **has** a slight limp.
> The only **one** of those guys who ever **says** "thank you" is Bluto--and
> he only mumbles.

1: Straightforward Writing is Driven by Clauses
SUMMARY AND APPLICATION NOTES

Summary:

An important mindset: Think of everything you write--that report, that memo, that proposal--as a story. Any story contains *characters* (people, or living or inanimate things) who act, are acted upon or are described. Any story must make clear exactly who those characters and what those actions are, then move the reader forward from start to finish as effortlessly as possible.

Only a *clause* (a group of words with both subject and verb) can carry a complete thought. Only a clause can tell at one time what is happening, to whom or to what it happens, and when. It is the core ingredient of Straightforward Writing. Use clauses copiously.

An *independent* clause can stand alone. When it does it becomes a sentence. Or it can form a sentence by adding *dependent* clauses that rely on this main clause to complete their meaning. Each of those will have a grammatical *name*--a part of speech (noun, pronoun, adverb, adjective)--and do the same *job* that a single word with that name would.

The core word in the subject (the *simple subject*) determines the verb and whether that verb is singular or plural. So always keep track of your simple subject.

Application Notes:

Used with skill, clauses can drive your writing on a straightforward path. *(Clause-driven writing.)* But if you let them default on their job, they will have to be dragged along by the rest of your language. *(Clause-dragging writing.)*

Here's how to take advantage of clause power:

1. First, begin to look for--to *think* in--noun-verb or pronoun-verb combinations to convey your message. *Use them for as much of the message as you can.* **Don't be afraid you'll overdo.** *You won't.*

You will soon learn to spot characters and actions hiding in phrases or, more likely, to infer what they might be. This scientist's clause-dragging version makes do with just two clauses (subjects and verbs underlined:)

Along the bottoms of some salt lagoons <u>are found</u> layered <u>communities</u> of bacteria called microbial mats, in existence for 3.5 million years, back to an age predating the habitation of the earth by animals. The microbial <u>mats</u> <u>are</u> diverse and brilliant in coloration, with a hard gelatinous surface.

From the above you may pick out, or invent, combinations from which to pick and choose, such as: *These <u>communities</u> **coat/cover/ clothe/festoon** the bottoms...The <u>mats</u> **gleam/glisten/shine/glow** ... <u>They feel</u> like gelatin...<u>They</u> **provide/offer/give** a look back, before <u>animals</u> **arrived/appeared/came** ...The <u>mats</u> **predated** animals...<u>Scientists now can look</u> back....*

One possible four-clause result:

> *Microbial <u>mats</u>--layered communities of bacteria--<u>coat</u> the bottom of some salt lagoons. To the eye, <u>they</u> <u>gleam</u> in vivid hues. To the hand, <u>they</u> <u>feel</u> like a hard jello. To a scientist, <u>they</u> <u>offer</u> a look back 3.5 billion years, to a time before <u>animals</u> <u>arrived.</u>*

2. Second, make sure that your subjects and verbs are the real characters and actions you are writing about, and not generalities or unpicturable abstractions.

Here the clause subject and verb (underlined) are certainly not the real characters and actions:

> *<u>The following</u> <u>are included</u> among our self-evident truths: the equality of creation of all humans and their endowment by the Creator with certain inalienable rights. (One clause.)*

At least Thomas Jefferson didn't think so. Subjects and verbs again underlined:

> *<u>We</u> <u>hold</u> these truths to be self-evident, that all <u>men</u> <u>are created</u> equal; that <u>they</u> <u>are endowed</u> by their Creator with certain inalienable rights. (Three clauses.)*

In addition to its powerful forward movement, clause-driven writing has valuable byproducts: Your message becomes more concise. Your writing becomes less abstract.

A

CLAUSE-DRAGGING:

Our typical <u>reader</u>, based on our knowledge of the credit union movement, <u>may be envisioned</u> as John Doe, a plant employee <u>part</u> of whose spare time <u>is spent</u> in the administration of the affairs of his plant credit union, in return for a small stipend. A high-school graduate with a couple of completed evening courses to his credit, <u>he is married</u> with two children and <u>is</u> a homeowner. **(Three clauses, 69 words)**

CLAUSE-DRIVEN:

What <u>we know</u> of the credit union movement <u>suggests</u> that our typical <u>reader is</u> John Doe, a plant employee <u>who administers the affairs</u> of his plant credit union in part of his spare time, for which <u>he receives</u> a small stipend. <u>He is</u> a high-school graduate, <u>has completed</u> a couple of evening courses, <u>has</u> a wife and two children, and <u>owns</u> his home. **(Six clauses, 64 words)**

B

CLAUSE-DRAGGING:

Although <u>it would have been</u> possible for me to write a summary on the exact identity of persons under indictment, concluding with a 10-point program for assuring honest behavior in the future on the part of civic officials, <u>I chose</u> instead an interview with the family of a police officer <u>who had been discharged</u> for allegedly accepting bribes. **(Three clauses, 59 words)**

CLAUSE-DRIVEN:

<u>I could have described</u> just <u>who had been indicted</u>. <u>I could have ended</u> with a 10-point program to assure that civic <u>officials would behave</u> honestly from now on. But <u>I didn't</u>. Instead <u>I interviewed</u> the family of a police officer <u>who had lost</u> his job because <u>he</u> allegedly <u>took</u> bribes. **(Eight clauses, 52 words)**

C

CLAUSE-DRAGGING:

That tree growth <u>rate is</u> not as rapid as <u>it</u> formerly <u>was is</u> common knowledge among residents of Boston and Baltimore, whose <u>belief is corroborated</u> by research <u>that has been done</u> in those cities on the annual-growth rings of trees. **(Four clauses, 41 words)**

CLAUSE-DRIVEN:

<u>People who live</u> in Boston and Baltimore <u>know</u> that <u>trees aren't growing</u> there as fast as <u>they used to</u>, and <u>prove</u> it by the work <u>researchers</u> in those cities <u>have done</u> on the trees' annual-growth rings. **(Five clauses, 37 words)**

D

CLAUSE-DRAGGING:

The <u>City requires</u> a topographical survey of a planned unit development having any portion of a site with a grade in excess of 23 degrees as determined by known data. **(One clause, 31 words)**

CLAUSE-DRIVEN:

The <u>City requires</u> a topographical survey of a planned unit development if known <u>data determines</u> that any <u>portion</u> of the site <u>has</u> a grade <u>that exceeds</u> 23 per cent. **(Four clauses, 29 words)**

CLAUSE-DRIVEN writing has many valuable by-products: shorter sentences, shorter words, fewer phrases, fewer abstractions. In short, less line resistance for the reader as he or she moves from start to finish of your message. (Subjects and verbs underlined)

CLAUSE-DRAGGING:

The issue raised by developers is whether this material needs to be provided with the initial design of the subdivision or whether it can be provided after tentative approval. The City's position continues to be that once tentative approval has been given, there should be no surprises and therefore sufficient information needs to be provided for evaluation prior to the public hearing and tentative approval.

A great majority of these cases are appealed to City Council with appellants having hired their own geotechnical engineers, a procedure made far less likely when community awareness of the City Review Staff's requirement for and evaluation of appropriate data exists. **(Nine clauses, 106 words)**

CLAUSE-DRIVEN:

Developers have asked whether this material must accompany the initial subdivision design or whether it may follow tentative design approval. The City continues to hold that there should be no surprises after it has tentatively approved the design. Therefore, developers must include adequate information for evaluation before the public hearing is held and the design is tentatively approved.

In most cases developers hire their own geotechnical engineers and appeal the cases to City Council. They are less likely to do this if the community knows the City Review Staff has required and reviewed the appropriate data. **(Thirteen clauses, 96 words)**

CLAUSE-DRAGGING:

A stiff magma with a consistency resembling that of modeling clay used in kindergarten is produced by the melting of rhyolite. Remaining in a dry condition, rhyolite magma is relatively harmless, and in quiet eruption produces thick obsidian lava flows or plug domes. But if absorption of water is allowed, and rhyolite's ability for such absorption is much greater than either basalt or andesite, the volcano is converted into a giant steam boiler at a temperature of about 850° centigrade, the melting point of rhyolite.

The sole gravitational impediment to its violent eruption is the weight of the overlying rock, and once eruption of such a volcano begins the lid is off and the entire magma chamber may be regurgitated through the vent in a blast of steam and shredded rhyolite magma sending clouds of ash high into the sky and covering the countryside with a blanket of steaming ash and pumice. **(Nine clauses,154 words)**

CLAUSE-DRIVEN:

When rhyolite melts it produces a magma about as stiff as the modeling clay kindergartners use. If it stays dry, rhyolite magma is fairly harmless. It erupts quietly and produces thick obsidian lava flows or plug domes. But it can absorb much more water than either basalt or andesite; if it is allowed to do so, the volcano turns into a giant steam boiler at about 850° centigrade, the point at which rhyolite melts.

All that holds it down is the weight of the overlying rock. Once such a volcano erupts, that lid blows off. The volcano may vomit its whole magma chamber through the vent, and the blast of steam and shredded rhyolite magma propel clouds of ash high into the sky and blanket the countryside with steaming ash and pumice. **(Sixteen clauses, 134 words)**

A Clause Worksheet

RECAP: A clause is a group of words, with both subject and verb, that does one of two things:

☞ It makes a complete statement on its own, independent of any other language; or

☞ It becomes a single part of speech--a noun or pronoun, an adjective or an adverb--and either modifies or becomes part of another clause. It depends on that clause for its meaning.

THE INDEPENDENT CLAUSE stands alone, and can be a sentence. Often it is:

Go! (*strictly speaking*, You go!)
You rang?
The corporation was dissolved.
Lulu shot Johnny.

The clause, as you see, can be a command, a statement or a question. It can run to any length, picking up modifiers as it goes along. In effective writing, those modifiers ought not break up the clause itself.

Tired of his endless trips to the corner tavern, where he assured her that he was only making phone calls to his cousin Rupert in Nova Scotia, **Lulu shot Johnny,** knowing that she would regret it later.

When the clause is broken up, so is the reader's attention:

Lulu, a hot-headed young lady upset because her favorite volleyball team had lost its championship game, **shot** her much-beloved **Johnny.**

Notice that the modifiers are mostly not single words but phrases and other clauses--each playing the role of some part of speech. The modifying clauses are circled or underlined. Note that each has a subject and a verb, and that some clauses contain others.

Tired of his endless trips to the corner tavern, where he assured her that he was only making phone calls to his cousin Rupert in Nova Scotia, **Lulu shot Johnny,** knowing that she would regret it later.

The modifying clauses are:

where he assured her that he was only making phone calls. (*Contains another clause*: that he was only making phone calls.)

that she would regret it later.

Approaching the same independent clause another way, we can mark off the modifying **phrases**. Note that each phrase lacks a subject or a verb or both.

Tired of his endless trips to the corner tavern where he assured her that he was only making phone calls to his cousin Rupert in Nova Scotia, **Lulu shot Johnny,** knowing that she would regret it later.

The phrases are:

Tired of his endless trips to the corner tavern (*which includes another phrase*, to the corner tavern.)

phone calls to his cousin Rupert in Nova Scotia (*which contains two other phrases*, to his cousin Rupert *and* in Nova Scotia.)

knowing that she would regret it later.

It would be instructive to mark both clause and phrase modifiers in that example. What it would show is that clauses may contain other clauses plus phrases, and phrases may contain other phrases plus clauses. As one example, the final phrase above, *knowing that she would regret it later*, contains the clause *that she would regret it later*. However, it still is a phrase since it lacks a subject. That is, we can't tell from the phrase **who** is *knowing that she would regret it later.*

The point is that, although a sentence physically is a linear series of words, grammatically it is no such thing. It is, rather, an often-overlapping network of words, phrases and clauses.

Your starting point is to get good at recognizing **clauses**. Let's look this time at two independent clauses--combined into a sentence:

> He was an Irishman from Boston without a nickel to his name, and she was his near-opposite, a Hungarian countess with a nickel to her name.

When two independent clauses (or more) are equally important, you may fuse them into a sentence. That used to be done more often than it is now. Today, it often works as well to use two separate sentences, since it is no longer dishonorable to start the second one with "and."

Not every "and," "but," and so on links clauses, of course. **Don't mistake multiple(compound) subjects and multiple verbs for compound sentences.**

> TWO CLAUSES: Me son Merton here is a good algebra student, **but** I can't say a single word in algebra meself.

> ONE CLAUSE, COMPOUND SUBJECT: The chief financial officer **and** one of his assistants were charged with fraud.

> ONE CLAUSE, COMPOUND VERB. The chief financial officer read the charges **and** spat on the floor, in that order.

DEPENDENT CLAUSES. The most common sentence--and rightfully so--is one independent clause. The second most common adds to it one or more lesser clauses that depend on it to get their full meaning. Each dependent clause is a single part of speech. Its **name** will be noun, pronoun, adverb or adjective, and

it does the same **job** in a sentence that a single word with that name would. Note below that we can substitute a word or two for each clause:

> ADVERB: He was definitely promised his raise <u>when hell freezes over</u>.
> He was definitely promised his raise next <u>Friday.</u>

> ADJECTIVE: The racetrack newcomer <u>who bets on a horse named Dobbin</u> is bucking the odds.
> The <u>unthinking</u> racetrack newcomer is bucking the odds.

> NOUN: I completely agree with <u>whoever said war is hell.</u>
> I completely agree with <u>Sherman.</u>

Now, to see how well you understand clauses, try your hand at these examples:

I. Identify the four clauses in this sentence. The easiest way is to total the subject/verb combinations.

> Although it pains me, I must inform you that you overstepped your job description as janitor when you blew up the plant to reduce maintenance costs.

II. The next writer, unwisely, interrupted the main clause with a lot of other words and phrases. Let's see if you can still pick it out.

> Now that he has retired, Professor Frood, a brilliant man who had an IQ of 170, could, for an amount less than his salary, be replaced by two graduate students whose IQs together come to 175.

III. Count the clauses in that one--the subject-verb combinations.

ANSWERS:
I. Although it pains me, I must inform you, that you overstepped your job description, when you blew up the plant. II. *Main clause is* Professor Frood could be replaced. *There are three dependent clauses:* that he has retired, who had an IQ of 170, whose IQs together come to 175.

CHAPTER 7

Your Pal the Verb

If the core element in writing is the clause, the heart of the clause is the (verb.) When you have mastered clauses, then mastered verbs, you'll have gone a long way toward mastering writing.

What makes the verb special?

For one thing, it is self-sufficient. A verb is the only word that can be a sentence all by itself. "Go!" is probably the shortest possible sentence. Any one-word command is a sentence (an independent (clause), as you recall from Chapter 6).

For another, it is irreplaceable. Clauses and phrases can substitute for nouns, pronouns, adjectives and adverbs; punctuation marks can substitute for conjunctions. Nothing can substitute for a verb.

Third, it's easy to keep track of; it retains its name when used in a sentence. Many parts of speech don't. A noun in use becomes grammatically a subject, an object (of one kind or another) or a complement. So may a pronoun or an adjective. But a verb is almost never called anything but a verb.☛

> "Edit your copy; then edit it again. Then edit it once more. This is the hand-rubbing process. No rough sandpapering can replace it."
> --James Kilpatrick

PART OF SPEECH	NOUN	VERB	PRONOUN	NOUN	PRONOUN	VERB	NOUN	PREPOSITION	NOUN
Fittingly,	the prof	gave	him	an F	(when) he	wrote	the essay	in	Finnish.
FUNCTION IN SENTENCE	SUBJECT	VERB	OBJECT	OBJECT	SUBJECT	VERB	OBJECT		OBJECT

Fourth and most important, it is the only element that gives your writing movement. Not only do verbs themselves impart motion; but also they have crossbred with other parts of speech to bring added momentum. The power of these hybrids has been badly underrated by teachers. They are (infinitives), (gerunds) and (participles.)

The early Romans must have known the verb was special, and honored it with its name. From the Latin *verbum,* it means simply "word."

Students often have a dickens of a time with verbs. I'm not sure I know why--unless it's because they are taught in such point-

---

☛Careful grammarians may call it the **simple predicate**, but that name is so cumbersome that it is usually not used.

less ways. We all learned that a verb describes "action, being or state of being"--from teachers not one of whom could then (or can today) tell you the difference between being and state of being. And, if a verb describes action, why is *explosion* not a verb? (Oh, I know--because it's a noun; we all learned that, too. But does that "answer" make any real sense?)

And, if a dynamic word like *explosion* is not a verb, why should a wimpy one like *involve* qualify? Ask any youngster to find the action word in the sentence: *The disaster involved an explosion.* Want to bet which one the little shaver picks?

Part of the problem is, we have overstretched the term "action," which invokes sense images, things you can picture happening: *Walk, run, sing, shout, look, wave. Catch (the ball, the flu, my drift). Pick (your chair, your guitar, your nose). Hit (the ball, the road, the spot).* But our worklives are not blessed with many such verbs. Our work is increasingly mental and verbal. It generates "actions" like *consider, study, judge, understand, determine, accept, apply, increase.*

But **whatever** happens in the sentence happens with a verb. That verb describes what someone or something **does** *(talk, walk, thinks, combine, continues)* or **possesses** *(has, have).* Or, if nothing is happening, the verb tells the **status** of that person or thing *(is, are, was....).*

Consider for a moment how much information a verb provides, all by itself.

It tells you whether something is occurring now, will take place sometime or happened in the past. *(Goes* is happening now, *will eat* has yet to happen, *sneezed* is over with.) It also tells you whether there is one actor or more than one. *(Sings* shows that one person or thing is the singer--the soloist, the chorus--whereas *sing* indicates more than one--the kids, the birds.)

And--very, very important--the verb by itself tells you whether the subject is acting or being acted on. *Considers, will go, is running (through his notes, down the government, a bookie joint)* all make the subject into an Actor. *Is criticized, has been chosen, was conked on the noggin* all make the subject into a Receiver. We'll be referring to the receiver as the **Actee**.

The verb alone tells you all this information; you wouldn't have to look at the rest of the sentence.

Any clause you write will fall into one of only five sequences:

58

☞ Actor/Complete Action
☞ Actor/Incomplete Action/Actee (receiver)
☞ Actor/Status/Completer
☞ Actee/Action
☞ (less common) Completer/Action/Actee

(A side note about the last pattern: Grammarians were first at such a loss to know how to fit it into their system that they simply labeled it incorrect. They branded it the False Passive. But writers and almost everyone else would have none of that; the grammarians were hooted off the stage. The pattern, which is now totally accepted, gives you this useful kind of sentence:)

We	were taught	mathematics
COMPLETER	ACTION	ACTEE

To look at examples of the other four patterns:

1. Actor/ Complete Action

The company prospered.

The sentence makes sense; the verb is complete. You could, of course, add more information:

The *large electronics* company prospered *in spite of the recession.*

2. Actor/Incomplete Action/Actee

Sluggo Dooley hit
The Department needs

Yes? He hit...it needs...hit what? needs what?

Sluggo Dooley hit   the bottle.
The Department needs   a revised budget.

> **GRAMMATICALLY SPEAKING**
>
> A verb that conveys action to something or someone is called a **transitive** verb. One that can not or does not convey action is called **intransitive.**

In those two instances you were left dangling, and knew something was missing. But sometimes you won't be; then the rest of the clause will tell you whether the verb is complete--or whether the writer had more to say:

The Boris Morris chorus sang.

That could stand on its own as a complete statement. But it turns out the writer had more in mind:

"You have to bear in mind that I'm a professional. A beginner such as yourself cannot expect to achieve this level of writing in your first half-hour. Remember that many great writers spend weeks on a single book. This is because a book has to be at least 96 pages long, or else it is legally considered a magazine article. The problem is that, except for appliance repair, there aren't many topics that require 96 pages."

--Dave Barry

59

The Boris Morris Chorus sang "Don't Bore Us, Horace" for us.

3. Actor/Status/Completer

This book is dry; even its cover is dusty.

Here neither the book nor the cover is doing anything; they're merely existing, the one in a dry and the other in a dusty condition.

That gawky chap is Frumpco's first vice-president--the first to be gawky.

Again, nothing is happening. The chap merely exists in a gawky condition.

4. Actee/Action

Current social trends were discussed at the meeting.
Current social trends were discussed by the group.

The sentences make sense, and each verb itself is complete--with or without mention of an Actor--*group* in the second example.

Earlier I gave you the first principle: Straightforward Writing is driven by clauses. Let's add the second:

> **2. STRAIGHTFORWARD WRITING IS POWERED BY ACTIVE VERBS**

Here is a sentence containing an active verb; that is, the Actor precedes the Action.

ACTOR   ACTION   ACTEE
Non-smokers resent "second-hand" smoke.

Here is another way to put the same idea. This one uses a passive verb; the Actee precedes the Action:

ACTEE   ACTION   ACTOR
"Second-hand" smoke is resented by non-smokers.

Both those versions are grammatically correct. But they have different effects on the reader. The active-verb version has fewer words and a directness the second version lacks. But other advantages are less well publicized. An important one for us is that **active-verb writing is far less error-prone than passive-verb writing.**

What does this next example mean?

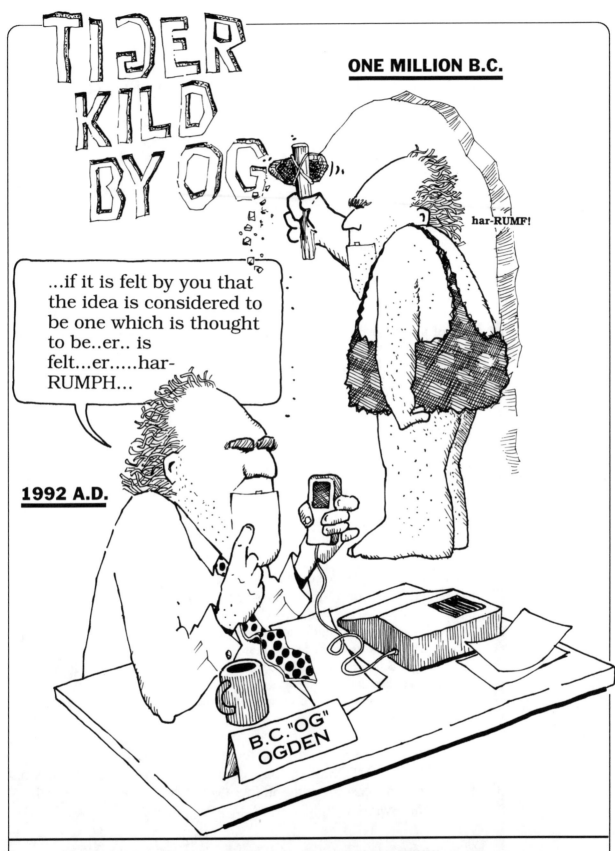

IT'S NEVER BEEN CLEAR why some people write nothing but passive verbs. No one has ever considered that it might have to do with heredity.

He was injured by the escalator.

Your guess is as good as mine. (Well, no; actually, mine is better, since I made up the sentence.) Was the person injured next to the escalator? Or did the escalator squash his foot?

Let's say the latter is true. The active verb--because it always tells who the actor is--would have made it clear:

> The escalator injured him.

If the other meaning were intended, your sentence could, of course, make that explicit also:

> He was injured near the escalator.

The dangling participle, phrase, clause--or dangling anything--is one of the most common writing problems, and one of the most embarrassing in that it often causes laughable versions. It is a frequent byproduct of passive-verb use:

> Weighing 600 pounds and made of concrete, the janitor was crushed
>   by the gate.
> (*Picture the morning headline:* GATE SQUASHES 600-POUND
>   CONCRETE JANITOR.)

Far more likely--as an active-verb version would have made clear:

> Weighing 600 pounds and made of concrete, the gate crushed the janitor.
> (*Or, equally active*) The 600-pound concrete gate crushed the janitor.

Passive verbs are like quicksand; once mired, the writer can easily get pulled down into further passives, and cumbersome language:

> Illumination is required to be extinguished.
> The man was ordered to be shot.
> Rounded Corners is planned to be converted into a private residential
>   community.
> The signature on the check was admitted by Fred Grunion to have been
>   written by him.

So active verbs offer you a degree of built-in error correction. But your main reason to rely on them is the contribution they make to Straightforward Writing.

Following are two versions of each of several passages. All versions are clause-driven. But notice the additional crispness and speed of the active-verb renditions--and the accompanying decrease in number of phrases. (Passive verbs are underlined--as well as all status verbs, forms of *to be*. Active verbs are bold-underlined:)

HARNESSING VERB POWER

I

VERB-PUNY: That a house or structure is an extension of our bodies, a new skin that is stretched out as a means of intercepting wind and rain and cold, simply has not been integrated as part of our thinking. (Three clauses, five phrases, 40 words)

VERB-POWERED: *That a house or structure extends our bodies like a new skin that stretches out and intercepts wind and rain and cold--that's simply not the way we think. (Three clauses, one phrase, 29 words)*

II

VERB-PUNY: Whether the workings of the biological nerve structure and those of a computer are identical is something to be discussed later. The point here is that the logical processes of the human mind can be simulated with speed and accuracy by the newest computers. (Three clauses, five phrases, 45 words)

VERB-POWERED: *Whether the biological nerve system works exactly like a computer is something we can discuss later. The point here is that the newest computers can accurately and rapidly simulate the logical processes of the human mind. (Three clauses, two phrases, 36 words)*

III

VERB-PUNY: In moister places the need to establish a deep root system is either less urgent or absent altogether. Perhaps for this reason the seeds of redwood and willow are small. And yet there are oaks in the eastern United States, where there is a tendency for summer rains to reduce this apparent necessity for a deep root system. (Four clauses, six phrases, 59 words)

VERB-POWERED: *Moister places lessen or eliminate the need to establish a deep root system. Perhaps that is why redwood and willow have small seeds. And yet oaks grow in the eastern United States, where summer rains tend to reduce the apparent need for deep roots. (Four clauses, four phrases, 44 words)*

IV

VERB-PUNY: A byproduct of the voter-registration campaign that was mounted for the poor in summer of 1983, Jackson found, was the creation of a substantial constituency of his own; as a result, a national arena previously closed to him was now being opened. (Four clauses, eight phrases, 43 words)

VERB-POWERED: *When he mounted a voter-registration campaign for the poor in summer of 1983, Jackson found he also was creating a substantial constituency of his own; it opened for him a national arena that had previously locked him out. (Five clauses, five phrases, 39 words)*

To summarize what you've found about clauses:

1. Clause-driven writing moves faster, is more direct and contains fewer errors than writing that is light on clauses and heavy with phrases.

2. Clauses powered by active verbs move faster, are more direct and contain fewer errors than clauses using passive verbs and *to be*, or status, verbs.

How to get into the active-verb habit? First, you need to recognize that it is a habit. More than that, if you trust your own conversation, it is a very strong habit. Consider these verbatim snippets from real conversations--one in a corporate office, one in a small-town coffee shop. As you read, "listen" for the active verbs. Hear how naturally they flow.

I First, I agree open-ended retirement has a lot going for it. For one thing, we could hold onto a lot of people who now are retiring that we would just as soon keep for several more years. And then there's the advantage to the guy or gal who doesn't want to retire. You know, a lot of people, right or wrong, do see work as noble. And for a lot of them it's the only chance they have for social contact...

But then you have to ask, how do you get rid of them when they no longer are producing, or we think they're not? Now we have an honorable reason: You're 65. And, face it; old people do get older; in that way they're a different kind of protected class. Women don't grow more womanly, blacks don't grow blacker. But old people do grow older, and eventually grow too old. How do you tell them they've reached that point?

II *I shouldn't wonder but what a feller couldn't get himself an old trailer and fix her up and not have to pay an arm and a leg. And when you outfit a rig like that with a propane stove and a bed, why, you got pretty near as good a place to live as you need, and it's got wheels to boot, so you live right where the fishing is.*

Now, again, with active verbs underlined:

I First, I <u>agree</u> open-ended retirement <u>has</u> a lot going for it. For one thing, we <u>could hold</u> onto a lot of people who now <u>are retiring</u> that we <u>would</u> just as soon <u>keep</u> for at least a few more years. And then there's the advantage to the guy or gal who <u>doesn't want</u> to retire. You know, a lot of people, right or wrong, <u>do see</u> work as noble. And besides, for a lot of them it's the only chance they <u>have</u> for social contact...But then you _have_ to ask, how _do_ you _get_ rid of them when they no longer _are_ _producing_, or we _think_ they're not? Now we _have_ an honorable reason: "You're 65." And, _face_ it, old people _do get_ older; in that way they're a different kind of protected class. Women _don't grow_ more womanly, blacks _don't grow_ blacker. But old people _do grow_ older, and eventually _grow_ too old. How _do_ you _tell_ them they've reached that point?

II *I shouldn't wonder but what a feller couldn't get himself an old trailer and fix her up and not have to pay an arm and a leg. And when you outfit a rig like that with a propane stove and a bed, why, you got pretty near as good a place to live as you need, and it's got wheels to boot, so you can live right where the fishing is.*

Unfortunately, we have not always carried this active-verb strength onto paper. Writing in business, professional and technical fields tends to be heavily passive, as well as laden with motionless status *(is, are)* verbs.

So you need to develop the same actor/action who-does-what-to-whom rhythm in your writing that you already naturally have in your speaking. It may take a little effort, but quite soon it will be as solid a part of your written personality as it is of the spoken you.

For practice, try converting these examples into active-verb sentences. Suggestion: Don't try a literal one-for-one verb substitution, but ask yourself in each case, Just what is the writer trying to say? and write that.

> The signature on the check was admitted by Fred Grunion to have been written by him. (*One clause.*)
> The necessity exists in the company for a more-careful analysis of the data. (*One clause.*)
> The number of his successes is equal to the number of his failures. (*One clause.*)
> Our shipment of the order must be delayed pending your completion of the enclosed form. (*One clause.*).
> (A tough one) As a result of Copco's expertise, management is provided with the ability to judge its future profitability. (*One clause.*)

Dum dum de dum de dah dummmm. (Sound of me humming while you rewrite.)

You probably rewrote the five preceding examples somewhat like this: (Subjects and active verbs underlined.)

Fred Grunion <u>admitted</u> <u>he</u> <u>signed</u> the check. (*Two clauses.*)
The <u>company</u> <u>needs</u> to analyze the data more carefully. (*One clause.*)
He <u>succeeds</u> as often as <u>he</u> <u>fails</u>. (*Two clauses.*)
<u>We</u> <u>must delay</u> shipping your order until <u>you</u> <u>complete</u> the
    enclosed form. (*Two clauses.*)
<u>Copco's expertise enables</u> management to judge its future profitability.
    (*One clause.*)

Reserve Power: Verb Hybrids

Here's a bonus section for you, revealing one of grammar's best-kept secrets:

Sometimes an active verb will not fit the sentence. In those cases you can often tap a useful source of reserve power--an assortment of verb crossbreeds that can put additional movement into your writing.

Feel the sense of forward motion in the underlined words.

> A visitor who <u>wants</u> to <u>go</u> beyond the guided tour <u>may enjoy</u> <u>riding</u> an elephant around the track.

> <u>Pushing</u> the dirt aside, bulldozers <u>clearing</u> the area <u>managed</u> to <u>uncover</u> the buried car.

Of those action words, fewer than half are active verbs: in the first example, *wants* and *may enjoy*; in the second, *managed.* But sense how much of the movement comes from the words *go* and *riding* in the first example; *pushing* and *uncover* in the second.

These words are an example of unmined gold. Because of their jobs in a sentence, they are not grammatically verbs, but nouns, adverbs and adjectives. Their names are of little importance to you; but the job they can do for you is very important.

These reserve-power words are called:

(GERUNDS and PRESENT PARTICIPLES) Think of them as *-ing* words: *Running, talking, eating, shooting...*Grammatically, gerunds are nouns. Grammatically, present participles are adjectives or adverbs. Neither is ever a verb.

(INFINITIVES) Think of them as *to* words: *to go, to eat, to discover, to examine...* Grammatically they may be nouns, adjectives or adverbs. Never verbs.

Because these hybrids lack verb credentials, most English teachers

BUM PUN

"Sometimes a suffix is employed to lend an important sound to a commonplace thing. The suffix 'orium' makes a swimming pool a natatorium. The day may yet come when a used-car lot will be christened an autotorium."

--Theodore Bernstein

overlook the power potential there. Their reasoning, as far as I can see, is: If it's not a verb, it can't convey action.

Dead wrong. Once again, feel the movement of these sentences, heavy with infinitives, participles and gerunds (boldfaced). Active verbs are underlined.

> To **drive** home his point, attorney Walsh <u>moved</u> toward the jury, **waving** the photo in his hand.

> He <u>intended</u> to **go jogging**, but, **hoping** to **avoid** bad weather, <u>waited</u> to **leave** until noon.

In a sense these *-ing* and *to* words are the phrase's equivalent of the clause's active verbs. You notice that, like an active verb, many of them can have an Actee--that is, a receiver of the action:

> To drive home--*what?* his point
> waving--*what?* the photo
> hoping--*what?* to avoid bad weather
> to avoid--*what?* bad weather

And in one other instance, the *-ing* word almost becomes fused to, and an extension of, the active verb *go:*

> go jogging

In a sense, these words moonlight as power-packers. Their regular jobs, grammatically, once again, are these:

∽ **A gerund** (or gerund phrase) is always a noun. It always answers the question "what?" It always ends in *-ing*. (Gerunds and their phrases underlined.)

> He enjoyed (*what?*)   music
>   his family
>   <u>running</u>
>   <u>operating heavy machinery</u>
>   <u>discussing the recent events in Europe</u>

As an indication of its unique hybrid nature, a gerund may be modified by either an adjective, like a noun (*better singing*) or by an adverb, like a verb (*by singing loudly, he annoyed his dog*).

∽ A **present participle** (or participial phrase) also ends in *-ing,* but it is always used as an adjective, modifying a noun or pronoun.

Riffling the typed pages, Hortense frowned.
Tells about Hortense

Clearly in a rut, Homer, quoting from Homer, swatted a homer.
Tells about Homer the ballplayer

☞ An **infinitive** (or its phrase) may be a noun, adjective or adverb:

(*Noun*) He wanted (*what?*) to try native foods.

(*Adverb*) Congress lengthened its coffee break to allow more free time between lunch and dinner. (*Answers the question "Why?"*)

(*Adjective*) His plans to convert okra into beer should keep him off the streets for a while. (*Tells about his plans*)

Now you know the grammatical jobs of these hybrids. Far more important to you is their moonlight job--injecting a burst of reserve power into your writing.

Look for chances to use them. Keep a lookout for common word combinations that they can replace. Let me get you started:

✳ Watch for words ending in *-tion*, especially if followed by *of*. This combination is often replaceable. (Active verbs underlined, verb hybrids bold-underlined:)

Application of cortisone ointment was recommended to us by the intern on duty.
(*Supercharged*) The intern on duty recommended that we try applying cortisone ointment.

Plans for discussion of the pending broom shortage before Halloween were announced by the committee.
(*Supercharged*) The committee announced that it plans to discuss the pending broom shortage before Halloween.

✳ Watch for "preposition sandwiches"--nouns flattened between two prepositions: *in favor of, in support of, in agreement with, in reference to.* Often they allow an infinitive substitute:

His vote will be in support of the contract and in opposition to Studs Mahoony.
(*Supercharged*) He will vote to support the contract and oppose Studs Mahoony. (*Note here that the common omission of the* **to** *makes the infinitive* **oppose** *almost indistinguishable from an active verb.*}

Attempts by Electrospoon for acceleration of the time-to-market in response to increased demand met with failure.

CLAUSE-DRIVEN FDR

Franklin Roosevelt was plain-spoken. A speech-writer's suggested line "We are endeavoring to construct a more inclusive society" got an FDR edit, and came out in his Fireside Chat as:

"We are going to make a country in which no one is left out."

Electrospoon <u>attempted</u> to <u>accelerate</u> time-to-market, to <u>respond</u> to increased demand, but <u>failed</u>.

✳ Also keep your eyes peeled for a similar replaceable construc-ton, *the_____of:*

the completion of, the achievement of, the acceptance of

Three weeks will be required for the completion of the annex.
To <u>complete</u> the annex <u>will require</u> three weeks.

The company attempted the achievement of a tough profit goal.
The company <u>tried</u> <u>achieving</u> (or <u>meeting</u>) a tough profit goal.

On your own you'll find other substitution points, places to in-sert these supercharger hybrids. In the examples on page 72, look at the extra boost they (bold-underlined) give the active verbs (un-derlined)--plus the increased conciseness:

2: Straightforward Writing is Powered by Active Verbs
SUMMARY AND APPLICATION NOTES

Summary:

The verb is the key word in writing, the heart of the clause. It is the *only* element that makes your writing move. Whatever happens in your message, happens with the verb.

A verb conveys "action," a broad term that also includes possession (*has, contains*) or existence (*am, are*). It may express that action completely (*He sneezed*).

Or it may transmit that action to something else or someone else-- an <u>actee</u> (*catch the <u>ball</u>, arrest <u>the motorist</u>*). Or it may just describe (*is, feels*) by being completed in some way (*is <u>happy</u>, feels <u>like a million.</u>)*

The strongest verb pattern (and the most concise clause) follows an <u>actor/action</u> (*The corn grew*) or <u>actor/action/actee</u> (*Our business needs support*) sequence. A weaker, less concise, pattern is <u>actee/action</u> (*The building was razed*) or actee/action/actor (*The market was cornered by the Japanese*). A third pattern conveys no action, but merely describes status or existence (*It was tall, This seems confusing*).

The surest way to immobilize a verb is to "smother" it by converting it into another part of speech--*discuss(ion), refer(ral), accept(able)*. The greatest difference between clause-driven and clause-dragging writing is this: *Clause-driven* writing emphasizes active verbs. *Clause-dragging* writing relies on passives, status verbs and smothered verbs.

Application Notes:

Once you've gotten into the habit of thinking and writing in noun/verb or pronoun/verb combinations--that is, clauses--the next step is to make most of those combinations follow an <u>actor/action</u> sequence (colloquially, "Who's doin' what to who?") Just as it is impossible to overdo clauses, *it is also impossible to overdo active verbs.*

Warning: The verb patterns of most business and governmental writing are heavily--and irrationally--passive and smothered. It may take an effort to change this pattern.

There are three steps you can take to become verb-powered:

1. When you see, or think of using, a passive verb, try to figure out who or what the actor of that action might be. There almost always is one. Insert that actor--unless doing so is awkward or contrived.

2. Begin searching for "smothered verbs," verbs lurking inside nouns, adverbs and adjectives. Once you get started, you'll be astounded how many you see. *Change as many as you can into verbs.*

3. Get into the added habit of <u>supercharging</u> your writing with action-packed verb hybrids: gerunds (**-ing** words used as nouns), present participles (**-ing** words used as adjectives) and active infinitives (*to go, to run, to talk,* etc.) used as any part of speech.

In a "smothered verb," sometimes you can't pry loose the verb itself. But sometimes you can turn it into a power hybrid.

For instance, *the advancement of science* may be changed into <u>*advancing*</u> *science,* and *for the promotion of business* into <u>*to promote*</u> *business.* Either change produces a more direct, more concise message.

Note below all the places (circled) where verbs or verb hybrids were hidden, ignored or made passive, and the actors suppressed.

After seeing the car she was being urged to buy at the used-car lot, it was obvious to us she was in need of a brain examination.

It turns out there are many places to substitute active verbs and supercharger hybrids:

When we <u>saw</u> the used car the salesmen <u>were urging</u> her to <u>buy</u>, we <u>knew</u> she <u>needed</u> to <u>have</u> her brain <u>examined.</u>

One more set of examples. First, note the buried action:

The ability of gorillas and chimpanzees to stand with their backs at a slant is attributable to their long arms and legs, enabling some of their weight to be carried by their arms and making possible balancing on their knuckles. This is exactly the position of a football lineman before the snap of the ball, or the position of a man leaning over a table. The progression from this position to an erect one is easy, and commonly demonstrated in chimpanzee behavior.

A verb-powered version would read like this:

The chimpanzee and gorilla <u>have</u> long arms and legs that <u>let</u> them <u>slant</u> their backs when they <u>stand</u> so their arms <u>can bear</u> some of the weight and they <u>can balance</u> on their knuckles. This is just how a football lineman <u>stands</u> just before the center <u>snaps</u> the ball, or what a man <u>does</u> when he <u>leans</u> on a table. It is easy to <u>stand</u> erect from this position; chimps <u>do</u> it all the time.

In addition to its speed, conciseness and power, active-verb-fueled writing--since it is grammatically simpler--will have fewer errors. Verb-powered language crackles with vitality, barreling along, carrying your reader effortlessly forward.

HIGH-OCTANE WRITING (and low)

I

UNDERPOWERED: Our hope is that commencement of shell construction <u>will take</u> place before the receipt of the architect's final interior plans. Otherwise there is always the possibility of the end to our good weather and unavailability of top framing crews. (39 words)

SUPERCHARGED: *We <u>**hope**</u> to <u>**begin**</u> <u>**constructing**</u> the shell before the architect <u>**submits**</u> his final interior plans. Otherwise we <u>**risk**</u> <u>running</u> out of good weather and not <u>obtaining</u> top framing crews. (29 words)*

II

UNDERPOWERED: By the State's not <u>having</u> taken into consideration these approved services during the calculation of the payment rate under the new system, the provider has been given a distinct penalty. In its lack of payment for previously approved necessary services, the State is not in agreement with the Federal mandate that the payment rates are adequate in light of the costs. (64 words)

SUPERCHARGED: *The State, by not <u>**considering**</u> these approved services when it <u>**calculated**</u> the payment rate under the new system, <u>**has**</u> distinctly <u>**penalized**</u> the provider. When it <u>**failed**</u> to <u>**pay**</u> for previously approved necessary services, the state <u>**disagreed**</u> with the Federal mandate that the payment rates adequately <u>**meet**</u> the costs. (48 words)*

III

UNDERPOWERED: Several meat-curing options were available for mountain families, with haphazard measurement techniques that, although they <u>would</u> probably <u>cause</u> shudders on the part of modern professional butchers, were nevertheless effective. Favorite meats of the amateur "butchers" then were hams, middlin' meat and, for really <u>going</u> fancy, the jowl also. Best results in <u>curing</u> were obtained when there was almost no time between slaughter and transport of these pieces to the smokehouse. Billows of gray smoke from the sides of the smokehouses were the official announcement of spring. (89 words).

SUPERCHARGED: *Mountain families <u>**chose**</u> to <u>**cure**</u> meat in several ways. A professional butcher today <u>**would shudder**</u> at the haphazard measurements they <u>**used**</u>, but they <u>**seemed**</u> to <u>**work**</u>. Then, the amateur "butchers" most commonly <u>**chose**</u> hams, middlin' meat, and the jowl if one <u>**wished**</u> to <u>**go**</u> fancy. To <u>**cure**</u> best, these pieces <u>**had**</u> to <u>**travel**</u> to the smokehouse right after they were slaughtered. Gray smoke <u>**would billow**</u> out the smokehouse sides to <u>**signal**</u> officially that spring <u>**had arrived**</u>. (77 words)*

IN THESE examples the active verbs have been underlined and the supercharger hybrids bold-underlined. Note the resulting conciseness.

CHAPTER 8

Nouns, Pronouns and Kin

Nouns will give you as little trouble as any part of speech. I can't promise the same for pronouns. Although they are stand-ins for nouns, they act up occasionally.

Noun, the first definition you probably learned in English class, stands for "a person, place or thing." A person or persons, generic or specific: *Man, woman, Betsy Mae, St. Nicholas, congregation, mob.* A place: *San Francisco, my home, China, Heaven, Hell* and *'Atsa Pizza Restaurant.*

That leaves *thing.*

Among the "things" a noun describes are birds, beasts and fish; natural resources and product names; crops, activities (*sports, sewing, yoga, espionage*); brand names; parts of the body; parts of a car; computer bugs; crawly bugs---and a whole miscellany lumped as "abstractions," things you cannot understand by the five senses: *Freedom, truth, management, problem, situation, belief.*

Nouns are the solids of your writing. They are the **who** or **what** that you write about. Whatever happens, happens with the verb; whatever happens, happens **to** the noun (or pronoun).

A handy test is this: A noun can always be coupled to *a, an* or *the.* No other part of speech can.

This test lets you pick out the nouns from even an abstract sentence like the following one (one which, I assume, means something at least to the writer):

> Interdependence of the various modes of correlation presupposes, as an initial premise strong cognitive ability and a high degree of synchronous intellectual activity.

An *a,* a *the* or an *an* could have fit in front of any of those words:

> The *interdependence,* the *modes,* the *correlation,* the *premise,* the *ability,* the *degree* and the *activity.* ☞

☞ Also, had some other words (adjectives in the example) been used in a different sense, they also would have been nouns: The *initial* (like a capital A *);* the *strong* (meaning those people who are strong *),* and *the intellectual* (that brainy professor). This shows that you can't tell from the word itself what part of speech it is, only from the way it is used.

A LITTLE GRAMMATICAL KNOWLEDGE is a dangerous thing. Sometimes you may have to choose between being correct and sounding like one of the guys.

Nouns are used in more ways than any other part of speech. The basic ones are as **subject** of a clause or a phrase or as **completer** of a verb or a preposition.

SUBJECT   COMPLETER
(object of preposition)

The receding **economy** in the first **quarter** depressed both our

sales and our **salespeople.**

COMPLETER   COMPLETER
(direct object)   (direct object)

Nouns also have these uses:

They can show possession (*the book's cover*) or act as adjectives (*tennis match*) or adverbs (*He worked summers as a janitor*). They can also complete other nouns or pronouns (*our sheriff, old Luke, chose me deputy.*) So they are very useful words.

A noun, like any part of speech, may be a single word--or it may be a phrase or clause built out of several parts of speech.

Arnold	asked	**forgiveness**
		to be given a doggy bag (*phrase*)
		that he be excused (*clause*)
Indigestion	is	**no fun**
Digging potatoes in the mud (*phrase*)		
That he keeps yelling (*clause*)		

As with verbs, the nouns that populate our workday lives are not the picturable ones used in textbook examples: *Man, car, dog, house.* They tend toward qualities, generalities and abstractions: *management, committee, research, service, marketing, personnel...* That can result in abstract and general writing, if you let it. So, don't let it.

Here are two ways to fight noun abstractions: First, look for simpler terms for the abstract ideas; second, insert strong verbs and supercharger hybrids:

> According to our investigation, disintegration of the compound is unrelated to air temperature elevation in the ambient environment.

> *Our researchers <u>conclude</u> that the compound <u>breaking</u> down <u>has</u> nothing to <u>do</u> with the air around it <u>growing</u> warmer.*

> Realistic portrayals of the lives and behavior of the ordinary population are not the sole achievement of art.

> *Art <u>can do</u> more than just <u>picture</u> how ordinary people <u>live</u> and <u>act.</u>*

A pronoun pinch-hits for a noun. Like any pinch-hitter, it is used because it can do the job better. "Better" in this case means more efficiently.

A pronoun saves you having to repeat a noun. A personal pronoun substitutes for a name. An indefinite pronoun is, as its name says, indefinite. What it substitutes for is usually not named.

> In case of global warming, <u>everyone</u> would get a better suntan.

Here the indefinite pronoun *everyone* saves you having to write out the world's entire population from Aabbenheimer to Zyzzcovich.

It probably would come as a surprise to most people that there are over 100 common pronouns. But the only real grief-producers are the personal pronouns, representing people--or personifications, like calling an airplane or Great Britain *she* or an animal *he*. The personal pronouns are *I, we, you, he, she, they,* and *it* (and derivatives such as *me, you, him....*and *my, yours,* and *hers*).

Some of the others might not be what you think of as pronouns, including *everything, many, several, few, oneself* and *another*. Since they behave like nouns, there is no real need to single them out. But if you absolutely are driven to tell them from nouns, our *the* test will quickly help you sort out the pronouns. Can you put a *the* before:

> people, either, no one, person, nothing, zero, few, neither, total, all.

The pronouns fall by the wayside, since *the* cannot fit ahead of them: *either, no one, nothing, few, neither, all.* But *the* works very well in front of *people, person, zero* and *total.*

76

I hope you're challenging the word *few*. Good for you. Yes, you can apply *the* to it:

> The few, the proud, the Marines *or* The Good, the Bad and the Ugly

And, because you can, that shows it is being used in this case as a noun instead of a pronoun. Just as *proud* is, in the same example. Normally an adjective, *proud* is used here as noun shorthand for *the proud men and women*. And *few*, normally a pronoun, here becomes noun shorthand for *the few men and women*.

Since pronoun trouble can cause an otherwise well-constructed sentence to run amok, let's consider the principal problem areas. Specific pronoun difficulties will be dealt with in chapter 13.

☞ **Wrong or ambiguous reference word.** Pronouns tend to attach to the nearest noun--which doesn't mean that the nearest noun always governs.

> The patient told the psychiatrist he had a bad habit--
> writing clean graffiti on walls. (*Which* he?)

Working around that problem, you might change *told* to a more-specific verb:

> The patient **disclosed/confessed/admitted to** the psychiatrist...

☞ **Imagined or absent reference word.** Be sure the pronoun reference you have on your mind also gets out onto paper. Sometimes it doesn't:

> Ringworm medicine has become so effective **it** is often treated at home. (*Unless you are indeed running home-tests on medicines, you need the word* <u>ringworm,</u> *or* <u>the disease.</u>)

> The candidates debated in front of the city's most-affluent citizens.
>   **It** was one of six meetings held..
> (*Revised*) The candidates debated before <u>a meeting of </u>the city's
>   most affluent citizens. The meeting was one of six...

☞ **Step-parent mistaken for parent.**

> The youngster was clowning, teasing his friend by standing on his head.

To help the *his* do single duty, reverse the order of the phrase:

> The youngster was clowning, standing on his head to tease his friend.

☞ **Following indecisive words.** *Everyone, anybody, each, everyone, no one, someone* and several other indefinite pronouns are really indefinite. They are singular, but they "feel" plural, making errors easy:

> Give everyone (*singular*) credit for using their (*plural*) best judgment.

If you don't wish to use the formerly okay generic pronoun *his* (and non-sexist writing should not use it), then your best hope is to use a Workaround and recast the sentence.

> Give them all credit for using their best judgment.
> Give each person credit for using his or her best judgment.

☞ **It is I, it is me, it is confusing.** "When you enter the house," one grammar textbook sniffs, "and your wife calls 'Who is it?' would you answer incorrectly, 'It is me,' or correctly, 'It is I'?"

Why, heh heh, we'd all give the right answer, "It is I."

Su-u-u-re we would! We would as soon be caught filching from the petty cash as mouthing any fancy-pantsy talk like that--no matter how correct it is.

But writing is not talking, and different standards apply, whether we like them or not. Status verbs (*be, am, is,* etc.) are non-directional, much like equal signs. (That is, *John is the president* means the same thing as *the president is John.*) *I am it* works, *me am it* doesn't work. Hence, use *it is I* and not *it is me.*

So, at the risk of sounding like Percy Stiffbritches, we may occasionally have to write wrong-sounding yet correct things like:

> There will be only we two at dinner.
> The best pinch-hitter left was I.

At other times, the wrong-sounding way is actually right. "Between you and me" may seem slangy, but it is proper grammar, and "between you and I" is incorrect. To see why, change "between" to another preposition--say, "for." If the phrase "for you and I" doesn't sound unnatural, break it in two--"for you" and "for I"--and you can see the awkwardness. "For me" is both natural and correct; hence, "for you and me" and thus, finally, "*between* you and me."

That brings us, at last, to *who* and *whom.* The same receptionist may ask, "Who did you wish to see?" and "Whom shall I say is calling?" Wrong on both counts--understandably, I should add.

78

(A commonsense note: You will seldom get chastised for using *who*, and often sound wrong with *whom*. So, rather than learn any rules, you may prefer to stick with the *who*, as a large number of people do.)

The simplest guideline is: If the word *she* or *he* would fit the slot, use *who*; if *him* or *her* would fit the slot, use *whom*.

Here are some typical questionable sentences:

> Ms. LeGrange, who/whom the hospital had said is unfit to resume full-time work...

> The brickmason, who/whom you blamed for the shoddy work, is in fact not responsible.

To solve these, it's best to Clear the Deck (as described in chapter 5) by first converting the questionable clauses into standard subject/verb/object or subject/verb/completer order:

                         SUB **VERB COMPLETER**
(Ms. LeGrange), the hospital had said **she**/her is unfit...
               SUB VERB   **OBJECT**
(The brickmason,) you blamed he/**him** for the shoddy work...

Reversed this way, the correct versions emerge:

> Ms. LeGrange, **who** the hospital had said is unfit...
> The brickmason, **whom** you blamed for the shoddy work...

Just one more benefit from having learned your clauses well.

Second only to personal pronouns as possible mischief-makers are relative pronouns. The most-used of these are *which, that* and *who*; their job is to tie a clause to a specific noun. In this bridge role they take on the meaning of that noun:

> The house that he built. (*That = house*)
> Is there anyone here who likes eggplant? (*Who = anyone*)

In general, *who* (also *whose, whoever, whom*) relates to people and *that* or *which* to inanimate objects. But it's a guideline only. If you speak of the dog *who* has just saved your life, or the company *who* values its employees, no one will fuss if you personify it.

A "rule" <u>that is not holding</u> very well (but <u>that I like</u>) is to use *that* to introduce a clause <u>that defines the noun</u> (there are four such clauses underlined in this sentence) and *which* to introduce a clause <u>that merely comments on the noun</u>, which this one does.

The most troublesome of the relative pronouns is *which*. It tends to attach to the closest noun--and it's generally intended to do that. But it also is sometimes used to modify the entire idea it follows.

It's better not to try the latter. But writers often find it too tempting to resist:

> He's always coming up with good ideas, which I like.
> *(Do you like the ideas? Or his continual coming up with them?)*
> He's always coming up with good ideas, and I like that.

> Miltie dialed the pencil sharpener, which was caused by his
>   poor eyesight.
> Because of his poor eyesight, Miltie dialed the pencil sharpener.

If, for some reason, you must use *which* for this overall modification, try your best to make sure it can't be read in any other manner. One way is to keep the *which* as far away from a noun as you can.

So, instead of:

> Yesterday morning he used FedEx to send me his marketing proposal,
> which I really liked. *(liked the proposal? or the use of FedEx?)*

> Yesterday morning he Fedexed his marketing proposal to me,
> which I really liked.

The flip side of the principle Keep related ideas together is one that says: *Keep unrelated ideas apart.*

CHAPTER 9

Modifiers; Fleshing it Out

Once you nail down your subject/verb or your subject/verb/completer, you have the skeleton of your clause. You can now flesh it out with modifiers. Modifiers are either(adjectives)or (adverbs.) Schematically, here's how a typical clause looks:

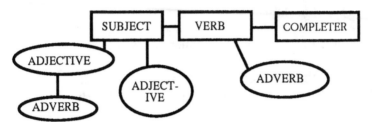

This may look simplistic to you. What about all those other parts of speech lodged in dim memory? What happened to all those terms we all sort of learned in school: prepositions, conjunctions, participles, interjections, gerunds, infinitives, genitives, exercycles, appositives, vocatives, presbyterians, inquisitions and those others?

As we've noted, a part of speech may name a word, or it may name a subassembly of words. (The clause is the final-assembly stage.) The above chart is at the subassembly level. Let's break down a portion of it (shaded) to the word level:

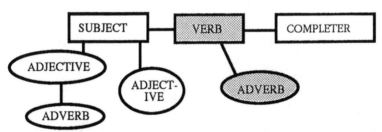

Once that's done, some of those other terms you were taught begin to show up. Let's say that the sentence represented by the above diagram is this one:

The very comprehensive Table of Contents <u>lists</u> the participants <u>by date and name.</u>

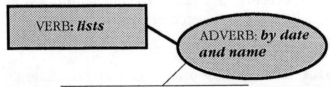

(**By date and name** is a prepositional phrase modifying the verb **lists**. It is made of the preposition **by**, the nouns **date** and **name** and the conjunction **and**.)

81

At the word level, all eight parts of speech may come into play. But by the final assembly level--modifying, limiting or defining a subject, verb or completer--you are working only with adjectives and adverbs.

Some of those adjectives and adverbs are single words. Some are phrases; still others are clauses.

SUBJECT	VERB	ADVERB
The girl	drove	fast.
The girl	drove	while she chewed gum. (*clause*)
The girl	drove	in a cautious manner. (*phrase*)

Everything in the right-hand column above tells something about how the girl *drove*. Modifying the verb, each is an **adverb**.

ADJECTIVE	SUBJECT	VERB
The tall young	man	whistled.
(*phrase*) Wearing a red tee shirt, the	man	whistled.
(*clause*) The	man	whistled.
who had just finished work		

The words, the phrase, the clause all tell something about the man. Modifying a noun, all are **adjectives** (pronounced ADD-ject-ivs, if it should happen to come up in conversation).

Of the two modifiers, adverbs are the more versatile. Adjectives modify only nouns or pronouns. Adverbs may modify verbs, adjectives, or other adverbs--even the clause or sentence as a whole:

The tractor moved **slowly**. (*Modifies verb* moved.)
He was **heavily** sedated. (*Modifies adjective* sedated.)
He was **very** heavily sedated. (*Modifies adverb* heavily.)
I **never** like to eat on an empty stomach. (*Modifies whole idea.*)

An adjective typically answers the questions: What kind? Which one? How many? How much? The adverb commonly answers How? Where? When? Why? To what extent? Under what conditions?

Those questions are probably helpful. But what really matters is that you **are always clear as to what word your modifier is modifying.** That will help you keep related elements together.

What demands the most care when using modifiers?

Placing them carefully. I didn't say just correctly; I said carefully.

MEMORY GIMMICK

Adverbs are the modifiers that **add** to the **verb**.

Adjectives are the modifiers that...um, er... well, that are not adverbs.

There are several correct spots in which to install a modifier, but some of those correct placements can muddle-up your sentences.

> (*Clear*) He told me on Sunday that he saw his long-lost cousin.
> (*Murky*) He told me he saw his long-lost cousin on Sunday. (*Saw her on
> Sunday, or told me on Sunday?*)
> (*Clear*) He saw his long-lost cousin on Sunday, he told me.

Clause-driven writing uses few adjectives and adverbs; that's one reason it has the pace and pizzazz that it does. Its specific nouns and strong verbs carry much of the descriptive power that we were told in school had to come from modifiers. (That **was** how that 500-word essay was padded to 1000 words, wasn't it? *The creaky, tired, wrinkled old man looked over the beautiful, silvery, flowing river....*)

Contrast modifier-filled writing and clause-driven, active-verb versions: (Modifiers circled, active verbs underlined.)

> Your (personal) opinion is (very) (important)
> What you <u>think</u>, <u>matters</u>.
> *Did you note the two clauses there?* **You** (*subject*) **think** (*verb*) and
> **What you think** (*subject*) **matters** (*verb*)? *If you did, you have
> a sharp eye.*

> (Possibly) to gain (their) compliance we <u>could give</u> them (subtle)
> encouragement.
> We <u>might nudge</u> them to comply.

Since clause-driven writing uses fewer modifiers, you need to assure that each one adds substance; secondly, that they offer your reader the least possible line resistance. So place them carefully.

Placement is less of a problem with single-word modifiers than with modifying phrases and clauses. Yet even lone words can go astray if the writer is careless.

Adjective placement. There are three locations for a single adjective. The most common is just ahead of the noun or pronoun it modifies.

> The **expensive** Hospital Plan promises TLC, which obviously
> doesn't stand for Too Low Charges.

The second common placement is after a status verb--one that shows being or seeming (in this example, the verb *is*):

> The **peak** that dominates the knife-edged Northern Cascades **is
> snow-covered** by October.
> (*Note that there is no difference in meaning between* the snow-
> covered peak *and* the peak...is snow-covered.)

As was true in the above example, there often is some distance between the subject and the adjective. I like to think of this distant adjective as a **wide receiver.**

The least common placement for the single-word adjective is after the noun or the pronoun that it modifies, as in this example:

> The voters, <u>divided and angry</u>, said "no" to every tax measure.

When the adjective is a clause or phrase, an after-the-noun placement is more common:

> The Sales Department, <u>acting as customer contact,</u> provides valuable data to our underwriters. (*Phrase*)

> Pre-existing health problems, <u>even if they are unrelated to the accident,</u> are covered. (*Clause*)

Adverb placement. Adverbs also work best just ahead of or just following the word they modify. But adverbs fit into more places than adjectives can. For example, they can attach to either end of the sentence. Sometimes that works; sometimes not. Here it does:

> <u>Scornfully</u>, the old man <u>addressed</u> the soldiers.
> The old man <u>addressed</u> the soldiers <u>scornfully</u>.

Just don't do that if you tend toward long sentences. You may lose the intended connection:

> The old man addressed the assembled soldiers who were talking to each other <u>scornfully</u>. (*What verb does* scornfully *now modify?*)

Remember also that an adverb can latch onto things other than verbs. A verb-adverb-gerund sandwich, for one, is hard to digest:

>   V   A   G
> He considered seriously revising his proposal.
> (*Better*) He seriously considered revising his proposal.
> (*Or else*) He considered a serious revision of his proposal.

Some adverbs are particularly unruly, and should be placed with special care. Probably the worst sinners are *only* and *almost*. Be sure you put them right up against the words they modify. Not:

> They almost hunted for six days. (*They never got around to hunting.*)
> I only eat Sicilian pizza. (*I don't drink it, or play frisbee with it.*)
> This hi-fi system can only provide a limited amount of power.
>   (*That's all it can do; it can't, for example, play music.*)

Remembering that an adverb may describe either the preceding or the following word, make sure your reader doesn't make the easy mistake of looking in the wrong direction. Which direction **is** the right one here, by the way?

> One person only can handle three responsibilities.

Does it mean there is only one person (perhaps Gertie) able to handle three responsibilities? Or does it mean three responsibilities are all that any person can handle? Or (c) neither of the above?

Is "very" a real adverb? Many good grammarians argue that it is not, in that it can't modify a verb; you can't write *The runner very ran* or *His speech very electrified the crowd.* So, they say, it would also be incorrectly applied to verb-based words. No-no's then would include *very pleased to meetcha, very relieved, very excited.*

Some bosses wield a mean red pen on this one. But hold fast. No, you do not want to apply *very* to a verb--nor to a word that might seem to be doing verb duty. But apply this test to the word you want to modify: Would it appear natural when used as an adjective in front of a noun? If it could, applying the *very* is beyond criticism. More words would qualify than not, including:

> very interested *person*, very respected *authority*, very
> excited *audience*

But these would not:

> very encouraged, very appreciated, very complimented, very loved

You would have to use *very much* in those instances.

Awkward adverbs. Adjectives ending in "y" make poor adverbs. *Funny, ugly, unruly, friendly.* Forget rules; don't write *He performed funnily, it grimaced uglily, they spoke friendlily.* Yes, those are real words. No, you ought not use them--nor should you employ adjectives instead, which sound just as bad: *They spoke friendly, it grimaced ugly, he performed funny.*

Then what do you do? Work around the problem:

> He gave a funny performance, it grimaced in an ugly way, they
> were friendly when they spoke.

Wrong adverbs for right adjectives. Most adverbs, although by no means all, end in *-ly.* The ones that don't are common enough so

"It is wise not to violate the rules, until you know how to observe them."

--T.S. Eliot

85

All politicians,

who are rotten scoundrels,

should be thrown out of office...

THE FACT THAT IT'S punctuated wrong doesn't always make a message less effective.

you won't mistakenly use adjectives in their place. But there is one source of confusion between the two.

Some kids who were nagged to stop saying wrong things like "He played bad" and "She did real nice" have grown into adults who will write, incorrectly, *I feel badly about your father's lumbago* or even *You looked very nicely last evening.*

The problem is that a handful of verbs--including *look, feel, grow, turn* and *taste*--have two faces. One, they transmit action from Actor to Actee:

> <u>look</u> the place over, <u>feel</u> the material, <u>grow</u> crops, <u>turn</u> the key, <u>taste</u> the pastafazool.

There they may be modified only by adverbs. But in another guise, these same words are incapable of transmitting action, and are very close in feel to *am, is, were, seem, appear* and other status verbs. Like them, these verbs must be followed, if at all, by adjectives:

> <u>look</u> beautiful, <u>feel</u> healthy, <u>grow</u> tall, <u>turn</u> sour, <u>taste</u> sweet.

Some purists argue that *feel*, for instance, does convey action, and that "I feel badly about it" is correct. But if you substitute any other adverb for *badly*, their argument falls flat. You would not say, "I feel distressedly about it" or "She felt stupidly about mistaking Tim Conway for Gorbachev."

Would you never use "I feel badly?" Yes, in one instance, to show intensity. "I feel badly the need for a chocolate soda."

Nouns used as adjectives. Some grammarians go into tizzies over noun modifiers used as adjectives: *Game plan, public opinion survey, government employee.* They will just have to continue their tizzies. Not only are noun modifiers useful; they have been an accepted part of our language for many decades. Where would we be without *phone conversation, peace treaty, music critic, city slicker*--and thousands of other handy and colorful combinations?

Piled one atop the other, however, they begin to lose their modifier feeling and grow heavy. A heap of them equals a heap of trouble for your reader. In general, more than two polysyllabic nouns in a row is too many, and can place great drag on your sentence. Try breezing through these:

> An automated general-purpose software incident reporting system requirements specification developed by a Software Center sponsored task group is ready for review and comment.

Provide critical survivability issue identification and survivability technology program definition recommendations.

Comparing adjectives. The standard pattern for comparison is to add *-er* and *-est*:

> <u>Big</u>, bigger, biggest; <u>old</u>, older, oldest.

But other adjectives--some because of tradition, some because of their length--work better with *more* and *most* preceding them:

> <u>refined</u>, more refined, most refined; <u>careful</u>, more careful, most careful...

A problem may arise when the two forms are mixed. Like the out-of-control broom in "The Sorcerer's Apprentice," an adjective preceding a list will keep working away, continuing to modify all items in that list until you stop it:

> (*Clumsy*) He was the most refined, cleverest and tallest person in the room.
> (*Better*) He was the tallest, cleverest and most refined person in the room..

An adverb is not a noun. A very common error is to use the adverb phrase as a noun. It's considered uneducated, rightly or wrongly, and an editor who jumps on it is correct for once.

> The best scene is when Romeo forgets his lines. (*occurs when*)

This misuse ranks up there with "The reason is because," which has been corrected (correctly) by thousands of teachers and is carried on nevertheless by tens of thousands of people who write. Don't join their ranks. It is an error.

Write thoughtfully. With care, you should have little trouble with single-word modifiers. However, when your adjectives and adverbs are subassemblies--clauses and phrases--placement gets trickier. The next two chapters should help.

CHAPTER 10
To Coin A Phrase

A phrase is like a clause in one way: It too is a related group of words that serves as a single part of speech. But it is very unlike a clause in the most important way of all: **A phrase cannot express a complete thought.**

A phrase lacks either a subject or a verb, usually both. That's why it can't convey a thought. To do that requires an independent clause, like this one:

> The space probe was canceled.

A dependent clause can't do it:

> Although the space probe was canceled....(*incomplete*)

Nor can a phrase do it:

> Cancellation of the space probe.....(*incomplete*)

Neither of the last two can stand alone. No matter how you mix and match, no matter how many you combine, phrases and dependent clauses fail to form sentences:

DEPENDENT CLAUSE   PHRASE USED AS ADVERB
Although the space probe was cancelled because of stormy weather that delayed the launch....
DEPENDENT CLAUSE

NOUN PHRASE   DEPENDENT CLAUSE
Cancellation of the space probe, which the spokesman had announced when the meeting began...
PHRASE USED AS ADJECTIVE
DEPENDENT CLAUSE

As you notice here, a phrase can contain other phrases. *Cancellation of the space probe*, a noun phrase, contains the prepositional phrase *of the space probe*, modifying the noun *cancellation*.

And even within that phrase, *of the space probe*, you find still another phrase, *the space probe,* used as a noun, completer of the preposition *of.*

The idea of phrases-within-phrases may sound confusing. Actually, it's much like the kids' game of making as many little words as possible out of a bigger word. The word CHEATS, for example, gives you CHEAT and HEATS. Then HEATS yields HEAT and EATS. Inside EATS you find EAT, and inside EAT the word AT.

That's just about the way phrases work.   Trust your own common sense; you'll quickly get a feel for which words naturally fit together. Take this sentence:

❊Because of a hole in the old oaken bucket covered with moss, the water leaked out.
MAIN CLAUSE

Notice that each of the following groupings in some way makes sense as a unit:

❊❊ the old oaken bucket
the old oaken bucket covered with moss

in the old oaken bucket
in the old oaken bucket covered with moss

a hole in the old oaken bucket
a hole in the old oaken bucket covered with moss

because of a hole in the old oaken bucket
because of a hole in the old oaken bucket covered with moss

covered with moss

with moss

By contrast, you can quickly tell that none of the next word groupings holds together as a sensible unit. Each is just a random chunk of the original, with an arbitrary start and an arbitrary stop:

Because of a

a hole in the old

the old oaken

oaken bucket covered with

So you see that the complete sentence ❊ above was made of one independent clause, *the water leaked out*, preceded by a series of word groupings, some nested inside others. The important thing is that it's easy to sense the natural groupings. Each grouping (other than the subject/verb core of the clause itself) is a **phrase.** Each phrase becomes a part of speech (its **name**). Each part of speech modifies a word ☛ (its **job).**

Now look again at the first list above (❊❊); jot down the word each phrase describes, tells about or completes.

☛ Or a word combination that we are used to thinking of as a single unit: top gun, jack of all trades, will be running...

Compare the words you marked with those on the list below. For each, I'll also give its **job** and **name**. Don't worry now if you don't know every one of those terms--we'll discuss them in just a few pages. The very important thing for you to learn here is that the phrase name depends not on the words the phrase contains but on the word it modifies, completes or tells about.

(*The full sentence again*)
Because of a hole in the old oaken bucket covered with moss, the water leaked out.

the old oaken bucket
the old oaken bucket covered with moss
Name: *noun.* ***Job***: *completer--object of the preposition* in.

In the old oaken bucket
in the old oaken bucket covered with moss
Name: *adjective.* ***Job***: *modifier of the noun* hole. *It answers the*
     question "Which hole?"

A hole in the old oaken bucket
a hole in the old oaken bucket covered with moss
Name: *noun.* ***Job***: *completer--object of the preposition* because of.

Because of a hole in the old oaken bucket
Because of a hole in the old oaken bucket covered with moss
Name: *adverb.* ***Job***: *modifier of the verb* leaked. *It answers the*
     question "Why did it leak?"

Covered with moss
Name: *adjective.* ***Job***: *modifier of the noun* bucket. *It answers the*
     question "What kind of bucket?"

With moss
Name: *adverb.* ***Job***: *modifier of the adjective* covered. *It answers the*
     question "Covered how?"

Here are two more examples for you to study. Mark off what you think the natural groupings are--remembering that one phrase typically nests within another. Then try to figure the **job** of each phrase. Is it an Actor? An Actee (receiver of action)? A Completer of a verb? If it is a Modifier, what word is it telling you more about? I've underlined each clause's simple subject and verb.

     1. The purpose of this design methodology is to ensure consistency of chip design.

     2. I have evidence to prove that Slurpees are a North Korean plot to weaken our spirit.

Okay. Here are some groupings that you may have spotted:

     1. The purpose of this design methodology
        (*Noun phrase.* ***Actor***, *subject of clause.*)

91

of this design methodology
(*Prepositional phrase used as adjective.* **Modifier** *of noun* purpose.)

this design methodology
(*Noun phrase.* **Completer**--*object of preposition* of.)

to ensure consistency of chip design
(*Infinitive phrase used as noun.* **Completer** *of verb* is.)

consistency of chip design
(*Noun phrase.* **Actee**, *receives action of infinitive* to ensure.)

of chip design
(*Prepositional phrase used as adjective.* **Modifier** *of noun* consistency.)

2. I have evidence
(*Independent clause, main thought of sentence.*)

evidence to prove that Slurpees are a North Korean plot to weaken
our spirit.
(*Noun phrase.* **Actee**, *receives action of verb* have.)

to prove that Slurpees are a North Korean plot to weaken
our spirit.
(*Infinitive phrase.* **Modifier** *of noun* evidence.)

that Slurpees are a North Korean plot to weaken our spirit.
(*Noun clause--with subject and verb.* **Actee**, *receives action of
infinitive* to prove.)

a North Korean plot to weaken our spirit.
(*Noun phrase.* **Completer** *of status verb* are.)

to weaken our spirit.
(*Infinitive phrase used as adjective.* **Modifier** *of noun* plot.)

With a little practice, you will become adept at spotting phrases. Then you can break down any sentence by following these steps from the word stage through the subassembly stage:

•◆ Locate a phrase.

•◆ Determine which word it modifies or completes.

•◆ Figure out what phrase or clause that word is part of.

•◆ Repeat this process as many times as it takes. It will eventually lead you to either the Actor of the main clause, its Action (verb), or the Actee or Completer. And you will have analyzed in detail how the phrase you began with fits into the final sentence.

Let's run through this process using a complex sentence:

Although no one knew exactly, because of the sketchy reports coming in, the damage done by the Michelangelo computer virus must have been substantial.

Pick a phrase, any phrase.
> coming in

Determine which **word** it modifies or completes.
> *Modifies* reports

Figure out what **phrase or clause** that word is part of.
> *The noun phrase* the sketchy reports coming in.

See what **word** that phrase modifies or completes.
> *Completes the preposition* because of, *forming a prepositional phrase.*

Determine which **word** that phrase modifies.
> *Modifies the verb* knew. *(Why did no one know?)*

What **phrase or clause** is that word part of?
> *Part of the dependent clause* Although no one knew.

What **word** does that clause modify or complete?
> *Completes the verb* must have been. *(Under what conditions must it have been?)*

To what **phrase or clause** does that verb belong?
> *To the main clause* Damage...must have been...substantial.

So, step by step, you've made a detailed analysis. (The following pages will explain many of the terms.) To summarize:

Coming in is a participial phrase. Its name: **adjective**. Its job: **modifier** of the noun *reports*. *Reports* is part of the **noun** phrase *the sketchy reports coming in.* That phrase's job: **completer**--object of the prepositional phrase *because of the sketchy reports coming in.* That phrase's name: **adverb**. Its job: **modifier** of the verb *knew. Knew* is part of the dependent clause *Although no one knew.* That clause's name: **adverb**. Its job: **modifier** of the verb *must have been* in the clause *the damage...must have been substantial.*

That clause (*The damage must have been substantial*) stands alone and makes sense; it is thus the main clause of the sentence.

Since a phrase (subjectless, verbless or both) is bound to tell you less than a clause, good writing requires that it usually be used for less critical information; that it be carefully placed--and, most of all, that it be kept short.

Kept short for two reasons: So the mind may comprehend it easily, and so the eye can grasp it at one fixation, about six words. Since we read by meaningful word groups rather than by single words, this one-eyespan test is worth applying.

In clause-driven writing, what role do phrases play?

➡️They come in wide variety, and so can provide a change of pace from the subject/verb/object standard word order.

➡️They can provide information that clauses often do not. The clause usually answers the questions "who?" "what?" and "when?" Phrases are particularly useful in answering "where?" "how?" "why?" and "under what conditions?"

> In the beginning
> Under the stairs
> Burdened by 50 extra pounds
> To see her grandmother or a wolf, whichever one was home
> Singing at the top of his lungs

➡️They can help you avoid repeating a pronoun:

> She could play Mozart on the kazoo although [*she was*] only six.

➡️They can contribute to conciseness:

> [*Even though they were*] Tired of the game, they still kept playing.

> Even so, Wilson was an effective president.
> (*instead of*)
> Despite the fact that he was badly disabled, Wilson was an effective president.

➡️They can succinctly set the tone of the coming sentence:

> Ominously,
> With a sly smile,
> Discouraged,

➡️Perhaps most important, they can play down information that would gain too much attention if placed in a clause, or would overload that clause:

> A tall fellow with sandy hair, Morgan Murtz starred in the amateur play.
> (*instead of*)
> Morgan Murtz was a tall fellow with sandy hair who starred in the amateur play.

One formula for conciseness says: When you can, change clauses into phrases, phrases into words.

That's fair advice; but the key words are "when you can." Sometimes it is possible:

Is this clause-driven, active-verb thing some new fad? Note the writing of Pliny the Younger, 79 A.D. (Subjects and verbs underlined:)

"The <u>waters deluge</u> man with rain, <u>oppress</u> him with hail, and <u>drown</u> him with inundations. The <u>air rushes</u> in storms, <u>prepares</u> the tempest or <u>lights</u> up the volcano. But the <u>earth</u>, gentle and indulgent, <u>spreads</u> his walks with flowers and his table with plenty; <u>she returns</u> with interest every good committed to her care. Though <u>she produces</u> poison <u>she</u> still <u>supplies</u> the antidote. although constantly teased more to furnish the luxuries of man than his necessities, yet even to the last <u>she continues</u> her kind indulgence. And, when <u>life is</u> over, <u>she</u> piously <u>covers</u> his remains in her bosom."

94

The man <u>who had red hair</u> (*clause*)
The man <u>with red hair</u> (*phrase*)
The <u>red-headed</u> man (*word*)

But use that advice as a guideline, not a formula. The ideas in many clauses would be grotesquely warped by such shrinkage:

The toddler <u>who has not yet learned to lace his shoes.</u>
The toddler <u>unknowledgeable of shoelacing</u> (?)
The <u>shoelacing-untaught</u> toddler (???)

As for conciseness: Once you master clause-driven writing, you will own the most concise of styles. (Refer again to pages 53-54, comparing clause-heavy and clause-light writing; page 63, contrasting passive-verb and active-verb clauses, and page 72, showing the turbocharger effect of infinitives, participles and gerunds.)

Phrases, individual units of meaning, can enrich your writing in many ways. As you use them, remember:

➻ Keep them short--especially introductory phrases. Don't make your reader wait too long to learn the subject of your sentence.

Fight the tendency for prepositional phrases, each one brief, to link into long bumpety-bump rhythmic chains:

At the top/ of their lungs,/ the crowd/ in the square/ in the
heart/ of the town/ yelled their taunts/ at the king.

➻ It's best to deal with only one kind of information in each phrase: A who, a what, a where, a when, a why or a how. Mixing them can be done, but it takes some skill.

➻ Information in a phrase usually will have less weight than that in a clause. So deploy your ideas accordingly, with the less critical elements conveyed by phrases.

➻ Be careful when placing phrases. They are far more likely than single-word modifiers to lodge in embarrassing places.

Phrases fall, or are pushed, into various categories. What those categories are called varies with the grammarian. The simplest way to think of them is by the part of speech each phrase becomes-- that is, its **name.** Most phrases become adjectives or adverbs. Some serve as nouns or pronouns.➻

➻ Most books list **verb phrases** also--*have been going, will do, is eating,* etc. But since they are merely strings of verbs, we will refer to them together as **the verb.**

GOOD GUIDELINE, POOR RULE

It's good advice to delete **as per** from your writing. The term is awkward, it is curt, and it is not always easy to define. Does it mean "according to" (*as per John Sculley*) or "similar to" (*as per the attached sample*) or "as decided in" (*as per last week's meeting*)? Luckily, most writers don't have to define it.

But it goes too far to say never mix Latin and English. Avoidance of the word **per** can sound silly, as in:

The Soviet shoe industry produced about three shoes for each person.

(No wonder the system fell apart.)

Here are some from each classification:

ADJECTIVE, modifying a pronoun:
<u>Having misunderstood its title</u>, I caught cold at the nude painting class.

ADJECTIVE, modifying a noun:
John Wayne, <u>tall in the saddle</u>, also became wide in the saddle as he got older.

ADVERB, modifying a verb:
The tailor cut the cloth <u>to fit Burlow's potato-shaped body.</u>

PRONOUN, used as object of preposition:
She received a faxed valentine from <u>her one and only.</u>

NOUN, used as subject of clause:
<u>Fritz's having learned German by the age of nine</u> didn't particularly impress his schoolmates in Duesseldorf.

So you see that a phrase can play any role in a sentence that a single word can.

There is a more formal classification of phrases. It is not critical for you to know it, but probably valuable. Four phrases are named after the part of speech with which they begin: The preposition, the participle, the gerund, and the infinitive. A fifth type is unusual in that it is disconnected from the grammar of the sentence. A sixth is merely a shortened clause.

•◆ **Prepositional phrase.** Made up of a preposition completed by its noun or pronoun object, this is the most common phrase. It is not unusual for these phrases to account for over half of a sentence's words. (That is not necessarily a good thing, it should be noted.)

I chuckle when grammar books explain prepositions with parenthetical examples (*in, of, from, with, etc.*) That word *etc.* bothers me; the reader is apparently supposed to know from that list that the following, for instance, also may be prepositions:

aboard, according to, apropos of, as far as, contrary to, on account of, until, via, during, except, since, notwithstanding...

Four to six dozen familiar words are prepositions, but nine represent over 90 per cent of all prepositions: *at, by, for, from, in, of, on, to* and *with*. When in use, a prepositional phrase will always have the **name** adjective or adverb. This example has one of each:

ADJECTIVE   ADVERB

In the center <u>of the paper</u>, make a mark <u>with your crayon.</u>

96

Most prepositional phrases designate direction or location, time, or possession or source:

DIRECTION: from the east, toward the barn, above the house
LOCATION: in the shed, under the blue sky, in Arizona, aboard the boat
SOURCE, OWNERSHIP, CAUSE or REASON: of the President, from the Bible, out of the well, about the meeting, according to the reports, at his suggestion
TIME: in the past, during the recession, before the war
COMPARISON: like a whirlwind

The prepositional phrase can convey a very wide range of relationships. It is such a common part of our written and spoken language that you've learned to use it correctly most of the time. Prepositional phrases will cause you little grief.

That little grief will occur when:

✏ They gang up in strings or chains ("phrasey chains," if you will), creating what amounts to one long composite phrase.

✏ They are carelessly placed and thus modify the wrong word.

Here is one example of each problem:

PHRASEY CHAIN:
The source of the leak in the tank in the parts room in the corner of the basement at the Main Plant...

CARELESS PLACEMENT:
Wallace agreed to fly to Chicago and back just before coffee break.

2. Gerundial, participial and infinitive phrases. These all derive from verbs--and, as you recall from Chapter 7, can pack a good deal of verb power. They differ a little bit in how they may be used--that is, in their grammatical **names:**

✏ The gerund always ends in **-ing** and is used as a noun. That means it serves as subject or as one of a number of completers:

SUBJECT: Running a company was harder than he had expected.

COMPLETER (of status verb): His dream was singing at the Met.

COMPLETER (object of preposition): Faced with being tarred and feathered, he asked if he could do community service instead.

COMPLETER (of direct object): We heard Elmer Fudd exclaiming: "You dwatted wabbit!"

ADVICE FROM A HELPFUL HANDBOOK

"Always use an adjective when you modify a noun or pronoun."

Okay; so what is an adjective? The book explains:

"An adjective is a word that modifies a noun or pronoun."

✏ Participial phrases begin with verb derivatives ending in either **-ing** or **-ed.** They are always used as adjectives.

> <u>Tired of the endless tension</u>, the Runceys gave up city life and bought a quiet little acreage <u>nestled against the scenic San Andreas Fault.</u>

> <u>Speeding down the road at 60 mph</u>, the absent-minded professor realized he had forgotten his car.

Sometimes a participial phrase closely resembles a passive verb. Even if you get confused, it is unlikely to cause you to make a grammar error. But, there is usually a way to tell the difference between the two:

> PARTICIPIAL PHRASE:
> The candidate was <u>defeated but defiant.</u>

> PASSIVE VERB:
> The candidate was <u>defeated by a close vote</u>--close to unanimous.

Here's the test: Substitute a known adjective (say, *sad*) for the assumed participle. If the sentence still makes sense (*The candidate was sad but defiant*), you have a participial phrase. If it doesn't make sense (*The candidate was sad by a close vote*), you have a passive verb.

Some people don't recognize the word *participle* without its buddy, *dangling.* The two words are almost fused in usage. Although it is not the only phrase that can do so, a participial phrase sometimes either truly does dangle (is loose from its clause) or, worse, makes a bad connection. We'll say more about this in Chapter 13. Here is one example of a dangler, and one of a bum connection:

> TRUE DANGLER:
> <u>Shining brightly down on the desert</u>, the artist painted the sunny landscape. (*No word there for* shining *to modify.*)

> FAULTY CONNECTION:
> <u>Trapped in a corner after a long chase</u>, the huge crowd called for the mugger's arrest. (Trapped *hooks onto* crowd *instead of* mugger.)

✏ The infinitive phrase comprises the word *to* plus an action. It is versatile, and may be used as noun, adverb or adjective.

> NOUN USED AS COMPLETER (*object of verb*):
> He had <u>to quit reading</u> because his lips got tired.

> ADVERB:
> He walked <u>to get aerobic exercise.</u>

ADJECTIVE:
Binky's efforts <u>to win the spelling contest</u> foundered when he spelled "relief" R-O-L-A-I-D-S.

The infinitive phrase sometimes comes very close to being a clause. Note this example:

The CEO had encouraged <u>him to take early retirement</u>, at age 32.

Not only does *to take* have definite action, but the phrase, also like a clause, has a subject, *him*, as well as an object, *early retirement*. So you can see the close similarity between this phrase and a clause.

	SUB	VERB	OBJECT
CLAUSE	He	will take	early retirement.

	SUB	INF	OBJECT
INF PHRASE	him	to take	early retirement.

Admittedly "him" makes a funny-looking subject, unless you are Tonto. ("Him bad outlaw, Lone Ranger.") But here you see the hybrid nature of the infinitive. As the object of the verb *had encouraged*, the word has to be *him*.

Like *dangling participle*, the words *split infinitive* seem almost an unbreakable pair. We've disposed of the bugaboo about split infinitives way back in chapter 2. Forget about them.

⇥ Elliptical phrase. If you follow the advice, cited earlier in this chapter, to shorten clauses into phrases when possible, you usually come up with an elliptical phrase. Like the infinitive example just discussed, it is sort of a phrase, sort of a clause. In truth, it is a clause with some words left out (indicated in italics).

The hippo [*that was*] accidentally put into the bobcat cage did his best by meowing to please the zoo visitors.

The child, [*who had been*] reported lost, was actually off practicing transcendental meditation.

Elliptical phrases contribute to conciseness. Just make sure that they, like all phrases, are carefully placed.

⇥ Absolute phrase. Grammar changes mostly by popular revolt. If writers ignore a rule long enough, that "rule" becomes an option.

Sometimes new terms are added when old ones seem not to fit. The *absolute phrase* is a relative newcomer. It describes a phrase that has no grammatical connection to the rest of the sentence at all. It is almost a separate thought, patched onto the existing sentence.

AN UNKIND WORD FOR CLICHES

"[The writer] should take warning that when they suggest themselves it is because what he is writing is bad stuff, or it would not need such help."

--H.W. Fowler

Here are some sentences beginning with absolute phrases:

> The sky being blue and the air clear, we left for the lake.
> Interestingly enough, the Germans had no real use for the new weapons.
> More to the point, he was not the only one who had made the error.
> To continue with my story, Bill had fallen down the manhole....

You notice that the phrases do not describe or tell more about the subject; nor do they describe or tell more about the verb. The first one, *the sky being blue,* gives a bit of context for the main clause. The second, third and fourth ones are merely "asides" by the writer.

The absolute phrase is worth mentioning because it may at first resemble a dangling modifier. (In fact, many teachers used to confuse the two and mark students down because of that.)

Well, how do the two differ? In a simple way: The dangler leads the reader to expect, or look for, its subject to be mentioned in the next few words. An absolute phrase sets up no expectation.

> The sky being blue and the air clear,

No one would imagine that this phrase describes the subject.

> Interestingly,

Clearly this is the writer saying as an aside to the reader, "This is an interesting point I'm about to make."

> But:

> Deep blue and cloudless,

does call for a subject. What is it that is blue and cloudless? Surely not:

> Deep blue and cloudless, the jetliner sped through the summer sky.

If you were to revise that dangler, any attempt to keep the beginning phrase would probably be unnatural, like this one:

> Deep blue and cloudless, the summer sky was sped through by the jet.

So the solution here, once again, is to use a Workaround:

> The jet sped through the deep blue, cloudless summer sky.

Here is an example of two absolute phrases and two danglers. See if you can pick out which are which:

> Sure enough, there was Eddie on the diving board acting like a nut.
> Sure of his own swimming ability, the deep pool didn't faze Eddie.

MOST VERB-MANGLERS aren't aware that's what they're doing. But a few--repeat, few--do it on purpose. They figure that if they hide the action words they may avoid responsibility for the action.

The ugliest thing in the exhibit, Arnold found the sculpture strangely
fascinating.
For the last time, will you please pick up your old artgum erasers?

You probably picked out the first and last examples as absolutes,
the middle two as danglers--which could be corrected thus:

(*Dangling*) Sure of his own swimming ability, the deep pool didn't faze
Eddie.
(*Corrected*) Sure of his own swimming ability, Eddie wasn't fazed by the
deep pool.

(*Dangling*) The ugliest thing in the exhibit, Arnold found the sculpture
strangely fascinating.
(*Corrected*) The ugliest thing in the exhibit, the sculpture strangely
fascinated Arnold.

The absolute phrase is a useful element of writing. You are unlikely to overuse it or misuse it. Just stay clear in your mind as to
the difference between it and a dangler.

Straightforward Sentences

> **STRAIGHTFORWARD WRITING:**
>
> ➡ IS DRIVEN BY CLAUSES
> ➡ IS POWERED BY ACTIVE VERBS

You've had a heavy dose of content up to now. Before we add two key principles to those above, let's review the main points:

➡ **The clause** is the vital element in writing. By itself, it can be a sentence. Or, acting as one part of speech, it can unite with other clauses into a sentence. Every clause contains a subject and a verb.

➡ **The verb** is the heart of the clause. It describes what the subject does, has or is. It can describe that action completely. Or it can act as a transmission belt, conveying the action to an actee, or receiver (its object). Or it can simply describe the subject's status.

The <u>active</u> verb (actor/action sequence) gives the strongest and most concise writing. The <u>passive</u> verb (actee/action) yields longer and weaker sentences. A <u>status</u> (being) verb conveys no action at all.

You can turbocharge your writing by boosting your active verbs with verb-based infinitives, gerunds and participles.

➡ **Nouns and pronouns** are whatever your sentence talks about. They either generate or receive the action. **Modifiers** provide richness, specificity and detail: adjectives, which modify nouns and pronouns; and adverbs, which modify verbs, adjectives, other adverbs or entire sentences.

➡ These words are connected by others to form **phrases.** Like a clause, each phrase acts as some part of speech but, unlike a clause, lacks subject or verb or both. Think of phrases as the individual language "bites" that make up a clause.

➡ Every word, phrase or clause has both a **name** (its part of speech) and a grammatical **job** to perform. Sentences may be viewed at three levels: The **word** level, where words combine into phrases; the **subassembly** level, where words and phrases form clauses; and the **final assembly** level, where clauses form the **sentence.**

We've now arrived at the final assembly stage.

"A sentence is a very complicated contrivance. It often appears to have a life of its own. It will refuse to tell the reader what we know we have expressed in it, and it frequently delights in taking our most courteous thoughts and expressing them as if they were some sort of razzberry."

--Calvin Linton

At this final-assembly level, often there is no assembling left to do. Simply let the independent clause stand; with its subject and verb, it is already a sentence. **Use mostly single-clause sentences**; your writing will gain crispness, clarity and emphasis. Your readers will thank you.

But monoclausal (you should forgive the word) sentences alone just won't do it. For reasons of variety, subtlety or logical complexity, you will want to mix clauses in various ways.

The grammatical names for the various sentence types are not worth learning. And the quibbling about what is and what isn't a sentence rivals the philosophical argument about how many angels can dance on the head of a pin.

All your sentence needs to do is convey a thought. That's all. Sometimes the sentence is complete. Other times the thought comes through because much of the content is understood--that's how our language works. Below, the understood portions are shown in brackets.

> [You] <u>Get out</u>.
> Should we get a fax machine? <u>Yes</u> [we should get a fax machine].
> Three-dimensional TV will be developed eventually. <u>But not in my lifetime</u> [will that happen].
> And Dupin had the jewels all the time. <u>Very clever, these French detectives</u> [are].

That should take care of editors who are always on the prowl for "sentence fragments." Pshaw on them all.

To form a sentence, you need to:

➽ Select your main idea (main clause).

➽ Give it the emphasis it deserves.

Doing so will require links -connecting words of various kinds. Language offers us an assortment of them. My advice is to trust your judgment and don't get hung up on the "rules" for their use.

Some links are designed to show equal importance of ideas; some are designed to show that one idea is more important.

GRAMMATICALLY SPEAKING

Clause **links** include:

1. To show equal importance: **Coordinating conjunctions** (*and, or, so* and others).

2. To show unequal importance: **Subordinating conjunctions** (*because, since, although,* and others), **conjunctive adverbs** (*however, consequently* and others), and **relative pronouns** (*who, which,* and others).

They all do the same thing: Show the relationship between one clause and another.

104

Those intending to show equality of ideas are the fewer: *And, but, so, yet, or, for,* and *nor.* The standard practice is to precede the link with a comma, to signal that you do have two main clauses. (On very short sentences this comma is optional.) Or you can show equality by using a semicolon instead of the conjunction.

> Never eat at a place named "Mom's," and never play cards with a
> guy named Doc.
> Never eat at a place named "Mom's;" never play cards
> with a guy named Doc.

Or, for that matter, this version is no longer frowned on:

> Never eat at a place named "Mom's." And never play cards with a
> guy named Doc.

These connectors--period, semicolon, *and*--are really neutral. They imply no relationship at all between the clauses. The reader is simply allowed to infer what the relationship between clauses is.

Others of the above links do--or may--imply equality. They are *or, for,* and *nor.*

> He was neither a friend, nor was he an enemy.

To test the equality, we can reverse the clauses and have the same meaning:

> He was neither an enemy, nor was he a friend.

> They could play it safe and attempt a field goal, or they could
> gamble on a long pass.
> They could gamble on a long pass, or they could play it safe and
> attempt a field goal.

But use *or* thoughtfully. The same should be said for *and.* They don't always show equality, no matter what the textbook says:

> You come over here right away, or I'll box your ears and send
> them to Newark, NJ.
> He failed the driving test, and he was a Rhodes scholar!

The clauses are not equally important. Each sentence clearly emphasizes one over the other. The real meanings are (main ideas underlined):

> If you don't come over here right away, I'll box your ears.
> He failed the driving test, even though he was a Rhodes scholar.

105

"At times [the writer] may indulge himself with a long sentence, but he will make sure that there are no folds in it, no vaguenesses, no parenthetical interruptions of its view as a whole; when he has done with it, it won't be a sea-serpent with half of its arches under the water; it will be a torch-light procession."

--Mark Twain

ALTHOUGH FAT, GREASY AND SMELLING OF ONIONS, BUDDY WOLFED DOWN THE HAMBURGER...

You can combine as many main clauses in a sentence as you've a mind to. But your sentence can then become awfully long, and might better be reworded as separate sentences.

When you combine equal ideas in one sentence, the test for the link is: Reverse the order of the clauses to make sure the same meaning is conveyed. If it is not, you need to pick a more precise connector.

Just as each *and, or, for* link is traditionally preceded by a comma, those such as *however, nevertheless* and *regardless* are each typically preceded by a semicolon and followed by a comma.

> He was shy, but he entered the "Mr. Pecs" contest anyway.
> He was shy; nevertheless, he entered the "Mr. Pecs" contest.

Since these two categories often have the same meaning (for example, *but* and *nevertheless*), one way to remember the punctuation is to commit both lists to memory. Fie on that.

This rough rule of thumb will do: If the linking word is three letters or shorter, precede it with a comma; if it's longer, precede it with a semicolon and follow it with a comma. That is:

```
,SHORT
;LONG ,
```

Next to a single independent clause, your most common sentence will combine a main clause with one or more lesser ones. Thoughtful writing requires that you clearly signal to your reader which is the main one. Straightforward Writing says to go beyond that and give the main clause its greatest possible impact.

Each clause other than the main one will serve as some part of speech, and can fit against or even inside the main clause--just as it would if it were a single word. (Subordinate clauses underlined:)

> (*Preceding the main idea:*)
> Since he wouldn't be able to attend the actual performance,
> the violinist felt the least he could do was to show up at every rehearsal.
>
> (*The clause above is used as an adverb, just like*) Apologetically, the
> violinist felt the least he could do was to show up at every rehearsal.

(Following the main idea:)
On visiting day at the state pen, Butch enjoyed talking with his granny, <u>who will be released in six months.</u>

(Clause is used as an adjective, just like) On visiting day at the state pen, Butch enjoyed talking with his <u>imprisoned</u> granny.
(Both adjectives tell something about Granny.)

(Nested inside the main idea:)
The man <u>whom we now know by the catchy name of Tweed the Tailor</u> was actually born George Gabardine.

(Clause was used as an adjective, just like) The <u>renamed</u> man was actually born George Gabardine. *(Both adjectives describe the man.)*

The basic way to point out the main clause to your reader is simply to suppress the others. As we noted earlier, you don't make a clause dependent by taking away from it but by **adding to it.**

INDEPENDENT CLAUSE

(Because) <u>he was the chairman of the board</u>

DEPENDENT CLAUSE

Some of these add-on words merely connect the main and lesser clauses. Others also show the relationship between the two. Some are actually part of the lesser clause--its subject or its object.

The following links (underlined) merely connect clauses:

New York City, <u>which</u> the President visited last week...
I'd like the same dinner special <u>that</u> she ordered.

This link (underlined) is part of the second clause:

I'd like to catch <u>whoever</u> stole our tickets to the ballet, and thank him or her profusely.

And the following links (underlined) not only connect, but also show how the main and secondary clauses relate:

<u>Because</u> our town was so small, we lettered ENTERING REDNOSE and LEAVING REDNOSE on the front and back of the same sign.
(Cause and effect)

<u>So that</u> he could bite himself in the forehead, he must have stood on a chair. *(Purpose or reason)*

He was reportedly able to walk and chew gum at the same time; <u>however,</u> there was little demand for him to prove it. *(Contradiction)*

108

Now, to add two key items to our Principles of Straightforward Writing:

You can adequately identify your main idea (or your main clause) by clearly subordinating any others to it. But to give it added emphasis--and give less important ideas less emphasis--more is needed.

You have two powerful avenues for emphasizing or de-emphasizing an idea:

➥ By its position in the sentence.
➥ By the grammatical element that describes it.

↪ **Position in the sentence.** No position beats the only position. So if your sentence is made of one clause with no attached phrases, you have the strongest possible vehicle for your idea.

If your sentence has more than one clause, or a lot of phrases, the strongest position is at the end.

The second strongest position is at the beginning.

The weakest spot for a main idea is sandwiched between a clause or phrase at one end and a clause or phrase at another:

> While shooting baskets on the playground, <u>the Wilton youth was stabbed repeatedly</u>, according to youngsters who witnessed the fight.

> (*Strengthened*) Youngsters who witnessed the fight said that, while shooting baskets on the playground, <u>the Wilton youth was stabbed repeatedly.</u>

↪ **Grammatical emphasis.** Although you need to adjust this for other factors--such as relative length of ideas--the strongest vehicle for an idea is an independent clause.

Second strongest is a dependent clause. Third is a phrase--or a loose collection of single words.

> (*Independent clause*) Had Hollywood not attracted him, <u>Burton might have become the century's greatest Shakespearean actor.</u>

> (*Phrase*) Hollywood attracted Burton, <u>otherwise potentially the century's greatest Shakespearean actor.</u>

> (*Clause*) A popular manager, <u>Cooper had a loud mouth but a fair mind.</u>

"One very popular literary device is the simile, which is when you say that something looks like something else, usually some kind of animal:

'Winston Churchill walked into the room and looked like some kind of animal.'"

--Dave Barry

109

(*Phrase*) Cooper was a popular manager--loud-mouthed but fair-minded.

Combining these guidelines, we can see that--**second always to a single-clause, no-phrases sentence--the strongest placement of an idea is in an independent clause placed at the end of the sentence.**

It helps also for the element preceding that clause to be as short as possible--reducing the memory span required before the reader gets to the main subject.

And, although splitting a main idea doesn't always weaken it, it usually does. Especially if the intruding element itself is either very strong or very long.

Conversely, **the weakest placement is in a phrase or dependent clause, plopped somewhere in mid-sentence.**

Here is a strong clause-driven version, then a weaker one:

Jeanne Klieger's photographs proved Hammel was right when he revealed that the horrifying conditions prevailed even in our own town. (*Here the main clause embodies three other clauses--which is typical of Straightforward Writing--and saves the strongest message until last.*)

The correctness of Hammel's revelation of the horrifying conditions that are prevalent even in our own town was verified by Jeanne Klieger's photographs.

A further analysis of the two versions (subjects underlined, verbs bold-underlined):

VERSION 1: *Four clauses, three active verbs, one phrase, 20 words.*
(*Clause 1*) Jeanne Klieger's photographs proved
(*Clause 2*) Hammel was right
(*Clause 3*) he revealed
(*Clause 4*) the horrifying conditions prevailed...

VERSION 2: *Two clauses, no active verbs, four phrases, 23 words.*
(*clause 1*) Hammel's revelation....was verified...
(*clause 2*) that are prevalent....

We can now add the third principle of Straightforward Writing:

> **STRAIGHTFORWARD WRITING**
>
> ⇨ **MATCHES CONTENT EMPHASIS AND GRAMMATICAL EMPHASIS.**

3: Straightforward Writing Matches Content Emphasis and Grammatical Emphasis
SUMMARY AND APPLICATION NOTES

Summary:

Writing is part science, part art. Nowhere does the art factor come into play more than in giving your ideas proper emphasis. This skill has even less "right" and "wrong" to it than other aspects of writing.

But there are some pretty well tested guidelines to help you. Take them as generalities; but take them seriously.

The most intuitive (but least teachable) way to emphasize ideas is to use words in effective combinations. Why do we see "A thing of beauty is a joy forever" as memorable, whereas "Something beautiful is always a joy" would probably have been forgotten? Who can say?

But you have other ways to emphasize an idea. One is by giving it *a strong position* in your sentence. Another is by coupling it to *a strong grammatical element*.

Position in Sentence--

❋ An idea's strongest position is to occupy the whole sentence--as one independent clause, which both begins and ends that sentence.

❋ Second strongest position for an idea is at the end of a sentence. Third strongest is at the start of the sentence. Although most experts agree on this hierarchy, few of them offer any reasons. I think I can give you a couple.

A play whose second act is weaker than the first always has less impact than one whose second act is stronger than the first; Act 2 clearly has the more influential position. A sentence works about like that.

A related point: The second idea in a sentence, by immediately yanking the reader's attention away from the first one, risks diluting Idea 1. The worst dilutants--I call them dribblers--are attributions (...*according to Prof. Will Drone, who is head of the university's Physical Sciences department.*) and qualifiers (...*assuming that their figures are updated and have been impartially validated.*) Put them elsewhere.

❋ A third reason the end of the sentence has strength is that the closing punctuation mark itself tends to add emphasis to whatever immediately precedes it.

The weakest position for an idea is to be sandwiched into the sentence's midsection.

<u>Grammatical emphasis--</u>
A clause is emphatic because it contains more information than any other grammatical element. An idea gains most emphasis in an *independent clause*--especially when that clause makes up the whole sentence. Second strongest element is a *dependent clause*. Weakest element is a *phrase* or loose group of words.

Application Notes:
You can use the above information, of course, to play down an idea as well as to beef one up--or, just as likely, to make a clearer contrast between ideas. For instance, in a sentence with two content elements of unequal importance, you might choose to put the weaker one first, word it as a phrase, and keep it short; then put the stronger one last, as an independent clause.

Graphically, here is a spot-check of sentence-position strength:

Strong sentences, in order:

▬▬▬▬▬ MAIN IDEA MAKES UP ENTIRE SENTENCE

▬ ▬▬▬ MAIN IDEA COMES LAST; SUBORDINATE IDEA
COMES FIRST AND IS KEPT AS SHORT AS POSSIBLE

▬▬▬ ▬ MAIN IDEA COMES FIRST; SHORT SUBORDINATE
IDEA COMES LAST*

Medium:

▬▬▬ ▬▬▬ TWO MAIN IDEAS HAVE ROUGHLY EQUAL
IMPORTANCE

Weak:

▬▬ ——————— MAIN IDEA COMES FIRST, FOLLOWED
BY LONG SUBORDINATE DRIBBLER

Weaker yet:

▬▬ ▬▬ ——————

SUBORDINATE INFORMATION, MAIN IDEA, THEN LONG DRIBBLER

On the next page you'll see several examples of matching and mismatching. In some, the major ideas lose impact, or are diluted by others, because of poor positioning in the sentence. In others, those major ideas are well positioned as well as matched to strong grammatical elements.

*NOTE: This positioning (main idea first) is useful in the lead-in, or topic, sentence of a paragraph. That way the skimming reader, reading first lines only, can quickly grasp the main point of the message.

STRONG IDEAS IN STRONG PLACES

STRONG POSITIONS (underlined) WASTED

As much as 40 per cent of the waste in US landfills could be used to revive depleted topsoil by being turned into nutrient-rich humus, <u>according to reports from the Environmental Protection Agency.</u> <u>Composting</u>, creating an organic substance from grass clippings, leaves, kitchen scraps and paper and thus reducing the need for chemical fertilizers, <u>is a natural process of controlled decomposition.</u>

STRONG POSITIONS EXPLOITED

<u>Forty per cent or more of the contents of US landfills could be turned from waste into nutrient-rich humus.</u> The Environmental Protection Agency says <u>use of this material could revive depleted topsoil.</u>

<u>Composting</u>--a natural process of controlled decomposition--turns grass clippings, leaves, kitchen scraps and paper into an organic substance that <u>can reduce the need for chemical fertilizers.</u>

✍

MODERATE (main idea first)

<u>The best place is home</u>, no matter how many countries you visit, how many great sights you see.

WEAK (main idea buried in mid-sentence)

No matter how many countries you visit,<u> the best place is home</u>, although you may have seen many great sights elsewhere.

STRONG (main idea at end)

No matter how many countries you visit, how many great sights you see, <u>the best place is home.</u>

✍

WEAK (main idea amidship)

Because 60 per cent of American homes have cable TV, <u>widespread adoption of satellite transmission in the US has been hindered</u>, although it is popular in Britain and Japan.

STRONGER (main idea last)

Although satellite transmission is popular in Britain and Japan,<u> its widespread US adoption has been hindered by the presence of cable TV in 60 per cent of American homes.</u>

STRONGER (Single-clause sentence)

<u>The presence of cable TV in 60 per cent of US homes has kept satellite broadcasting from being as widely adopted here as in Britain and Japan.</u>

✍

STRONG IDEA EMPHASIZED

In this sunny, pleasant space, now surrounded by roses,<u> Christians once battled lions.</u>

STRONG IDEA DILUTED

<u>Christians once battled lions in this space</u>, which is now sunny, pleasant and surrounded by roses.

TO MEASURE YOUR READABILITY: The Fog Index*

The Fog Index of a piece of writing approximates the school grade level at which your writing can be understood.

To compute it:

Take a writing sample of at least 100 words. Determine the average sentence length. Count the "hard" words per 100 words--that is, a percentage. Count all three-syllable words or longer as hard except those that are capitalized, hybrids of short words (n*ever/the/less*, etc.) or made three syllables by adding *-es* or *ed*.

Add the average sentence length and percentage of hard words. Multiply by the decimal .4. That gives you your Fog Index for that sample.

FOG INDEX

WPS
+% HW
―――――
total
x .4
―――――
FI

Most writing done by professionals--who earn their living by what they write--has an FI of 12 or below. The respected Wall Street Journal, for instance, has an FI of 11. You should shoot for that, too. A 10 or under is considered easy reading; a 13 or above falls in the "Danger Zone," unlikely to be read--or at least understood. No professional writing is found at that level, although a lot of business and governmental prose is. Small wonder it so often leaves us mentally winded.

TO MEASURE YOUR PERSUASIVENESS: The Motor:Weight Ratio (sm)

Motor:Weight is the ratio of strong verbs to total words. Take a writing sample of at least 100 words. Count as a Motor each active verb and the verb portion of each active infinitive (*to go*, *to eat*, *to run*, etc.) Each word in your sample counts as one unit of Weight.

Do not count as Motors any passive verbs (*is discussed, was hit*) or passive infinitives (*to be hit, to be understood,* etc.)

MOTOR TO WEIGHT RATIO

STRONG VERBS
TOTAL WORDS

As an example: *I would like to go to the meeting.*

Its M:W is 3:8. The active verb is *would like*. The verb part of the active infinitive is *go*. There are eight words.

A generally accepted goal for persuasive writing is 1:10, one strong verb for every 10 words. As you master Straight-forward Writing, you'll do even better than that.

(For full descriptions of these two useful measurement tools, read "Write Smarter, Not Harder" [Twain 1990]. The order form is in the back of this book.)

* Used with permission of Gunning Mueller Clear Writing Institute, Santa Barbara, CA

Now that you know about clauses, active verbs and grammatical emphasis, how do you apply them?

Like anything, it takes practice. A good place to start is your own conversation, which is built on single-thought sentences and active verbs. Beyond that, clause-driven writing is largely a matter of mindset--learning to **think** in tight noun-verb combinations; asking of each element in your writing: Can this be turned into an active-verb clause? The answer is most often yes.

To get you started, here are some symptoms of weak, slow-moving writing. Each offers a place to substitute a clause.

❋ Possessives often hide the true subject:

> The conclusion from <u>our</u> research....
> <u>We conclude</u> from our research.

> Despite <u>their</u> objection to...
> Although <u>they object</u> to....

❋ Active verbs often lurk inside nouns.

> The <u>decision</u> was made at the council meeting...
> The council <u>decided</u>...

> There was a lack of any further <u>responses</u>.....
> No one else <u>responded</u>.

> My <u>writing</u> has a <u>tendency</u> toward <u>rambling.</u>
> I <u>tend</u> to <u>ramble</u> when I <u>write.</u>

❋ Certain preposition "sandwiches" are suspect, including *in_____of, in_____to, at_____of,* and *for_____of.*

> <u>In expectation of</u> a sales downturn, the sales promotion...
> The sales promotion, which <u>expects</u> a sales downturn...

> <u>In the event of</u> a decline in sales....
> <u>Should</u> sales <u>decline</u>....

> <u>In comparison to</u> the old quarters, the Center is structurally superior.
> The Center <u>is built better</u> than the old quarters.
> <u>At the request of</u> the Board...
> As <u>the Board requested,</u>...

❋ Suffix-heavy writing--clogged with *-ment, -ant, -able, -ton* and *-ency* words--almost cries for clauses:

Degrada**tion** of the signal is a typical but not invari**able** manifesta**tion** of electrical "cross-talk."
Electrical "cross-talk" usually but not always degrades the signal.

High academic achieve**ment** is not incompat**ible** with profici**ency** in prep-school athletics.
A prep-school athlete can also get good grades.

✽ Verb hybrids (participles) and (gerunds) have been praised elsewhere in this book. Much of the time, you can use these *-ing* and *-ed* words as power boosters. At other times, you can replace them with verbs, or reword:

Remaining in a dry condition, sulphite can...
When it remains [or stays] dry, sulphite can...

Exposed to sunlight for an extended period, the film...
If sunlight strikes it for too long, the film....

✽ Discard the standard wisdom that says to hold down the number of dependent clauses in a sentence. They can be very useful, especially those beginning with relative pronouns (*that, which, what, who* and so on); they sometimes produce a virtual cascade of information (subjects underlined, verbs bold-underlined):

I'm aware that, despite occasional disagreement with his staff, his pronouncements are genuine and his decisions **will be implemented.**
(*Three clauses, no active verbs, 20 words*)

I know (that) his staff sometimes disagrees, but he means what he says ; and what he says, goes. (*Six clauses, six active verbs, 18 words.*)

Which leads us--smoothly, I hope--to our fourth
principle of Straightforward Writing.

Too much of today's writing is abstract--nouns we cannot picture, verbs we can not visualize: *Management implements, research indicates, personnel evaluate...*

As I noted earlier, everything is a story. The reader of any message expects--**has the right**--to read about something happening, of actors acting, if you will. If he or she has to imagine the actor or invent the action, that is a tremendous deterrent to fast and retentive reading.

Nouns should be tangible, something you can touch. Verbs should be physical, something you can see or sense happening.

"A story can be wrecked by a faulty rhythm in a sentence--especially if it occurs toward the end--or a mistake in paragraphing, even punctuation."

--Truman Capote

116

That is not always possible, of course; but it is possible far more often than the writing around you would suggest.

Noun strength, in order:

1. People (that means pronouns have power).

2. Other things that in real life impart action--machines, animals, weather phenomena...

3. Inanimate objects that do not create action: buildings, chairs...

4. Abstractions--things you can not see, hear, smell or touch: *Truth, decision, approval...*

Verb strength, in order:

1. Physical actions.

2. Mental activity: *think, study, review, consider...*

3. Abstract verbs: *develop, occur, implement, corroborate...*

4. Status verbs: *is, were, seems, appears...*

Straightforward Writing says to **place your nouns and verbs in the highest of these notches possible.**

> **STRAIGHTFORWARD WRITING**
> ➡ **USES NOUNS AND VERBS THAT AFFECT THE SENSES**

Page 120 contains relevant examples. They are presented not as examples of how writing must be done, but of how it may be done. *I recommend that you also review the other examples of clause-driven writing on pages 53-54, 63 and 72.* They are directly applicable, and may be even more meaningful now that you have read this chapter.

4: Straightforward Writing Uses Nouns and Verbs That Affect the Senses
SUMMARY AND APPLICATION NOTES

Summary:

   Like most abstract statements, "Be honest" is something nearly everyone agrees with. That's because it is so open to interpretation. Does it mean, for example, never "borrowing" a pencil from the office? Some would say yes; for others, being "honest" stops somewhat short of that. After all, what's a pencil anyway?

   The problem with abstract language has two sides: (1) It conveys no picture to the mind; (2) it thus forces--or allows--the reader to create her own picture. The possibility for miscommunication is nearly unlimited. (What, as a recent example, are "family values"?)

   "The very worst thing about abstract words," wrote Robert Gunning, "may be that they mean nothing at all to anyone."

Application Notes:

   When your reader can see, smell, hear or touch your subjects and picture, hear or feel your verbs, you are writing with greatest clarity and most impact. *You can't do better than write about people performing physical actions; you can't do worse than write about abstract subjects doing abstract things.* Can you picture "Management's policy is built on respect for human individuality?" Neither can I, or anyone else.

   Some abstract content is needed in any writing--but probably only about a third of what is actually used. Learn first to think, then to write, in nouns and verbs that grab the senses and don't let go.

   Just how do you go about that? Here are some suggestions:

   1. Change activities into actors. Rather than "Research has indicated," try "<u>Researchers</u> have found." For "Science is discovering," try "<u>Scientists</u> are finding." For "Supervision is growing more difficult," try "<u>Supervisors</u> are having more trouble."

   2. Trust pronouns. For "Hamilton Corporation believes," try "<u>We</u> believe." For "Complete information is unobtainable." try "<u>You</u> can't obtain all the information." For "Should further information be necessary," try "<u>Anyone who</u> needs to know more..."

   Convert possessives. For "Our view is," try "<u>We</u> believe." For "Their position is that...," try "<u>They</u> hold that..." or "<u>They</u> contend."

   3. Unsmother "smothered verbs" (verbs buried in non-verbs). If you can, change "The agency's intention is" to "The agency <u>intends</u>" and "It is the preference of the court" to "The court <u>prefers</u>." Unsmothering does you most good when the emerging verb is most picturable ("In our upcoming inspection" becomes "When we next

inspect..." and "During upward movement of the market" becomes "When the market moves up.")

4. Turn abstract ideas into people--John Q. Public, our employees, the Average Man (or Woman)--or make them otherwise picturable: The Silent Majority, the Third World, the Evil Empire. "Today's city shows a meaner face" beats "The metropolitan environment is increasingly hostile." Whoever coined "trickle-down economics" gave the Democrats a truly indelible image; they should be grateful. (Less abstractly, they should say "Thank you.")

5. Try to turn abstract verbs into more-physical equivalents: "Squirm" for "have uncomfortable feelings"; "tweak" for "make fine adjustments in"; "knuckle under" for "capitulate". Great Britain has managed, if a bit inelegantly, to survive crisis after crisis. What better term than the famous "muddling through"?

6. Use concrete examples, either instead of or in addition to the abstraction they describe. If the subject is pollution, just what do you see, hear, smell? One urban planner tells us:

> Skies are clogged with grit-filled smoke that sears your eyes; buildings look more and more alike under identical overcoats of grime. You forget that the greasy yellow smear started out as a river, and that it once was blue.

7. Maybe needless to say, don't shy away from vivid writing. Its opposite is boring writing; your readers have too much of that already.

8. Finally--and allowing for very many variables--tilt toward the short word instead of the long. You'll be surprised how this simple strategem wars against abstraction and gives you writing that speaks to the senses.

On the next page are some before-and-after examples. Like all such pages in this book, they deserve not only careful study but also re-reading from time to time.

STRAIGHTFORWARD SENTENCES

(In each pair, note how Straightforward Writing moves you forward by using subjects and verbs you can see, hear, or otherwise sense.)

I. CLAUSE-DRAGGING, abstract language:

The natural turbulence of rivers enables some diminishment of this water pollution. Yet, the twin demands of a growing population are for an increasing supply of foodstuffs and manufactured goods on the one hand; continued construction of "septic tank suburbia" on the other. The waste going from a home with a septic tank into a sewer system is twice what it would have been without the disposal. Dilution of pollution is not the same as removal of pollution, and is clearly an inadequate solution to the problem. (*Five clauses, only one active verb, 89 words.*)

CLAUSE-DRIVEN, picturable language:

As they tumble over rocks and riffles, rivers can purge themselves of some of this pollution. Some of it. Yet, more and more people call for more and more cheese, paper and canned foods and at the same time keep building a "septic tank suburbia." Even a garbage disposal doubles the amount of waste we shove down into our sewers. Simply dilute the waste and what you have is diluted waste. You have really solved nothing. (Eight clauses, 11 active verbs, 76 words.)

II. CLAUSE-DRAGGING, abstract language:

That the current environment in urban areas is increasingly unpleasant is witnessed by the annual exodus of population from those areas, often on a permanent basis. The outflux of population is limited to those who are sufficiently affluent and fortunate. The rest are for all practical purposes imprisoned with no hope of escape.

The deterioration of urban areas is tantamount to deterioration in the very quality of life itself. Although cities throughout history have been stellar examples of civilization, storehouses of culture, providers of comfortable living and a catalyst converting individuals into communities, those important roles are gradually being diminished and replaced by an increasing image of cities as crime-ridden, decaying, characterized by both pollution and social unrest. The many difficulties faced by most cities, some far more traumatically than others, can not be explained by any one rationale. However, there is clear and obvious correlation between the disappearance of open space and the increase in these urban problems.(*Five clauses, no active verbs, 160 words.*)

CLAUSE-DRIVEN, picturable language:

The City today wears an ever-meaner face. It is turning into a place to get away from. Each year, millions of lucky people who can afford to, flee it. Some leave forever. The City too often imprisons the others. They are trapped.

As urban areas decay, so does the quality of life itself. Cities once shone as examples of civilization. They have housed us in comfort, showcased our culture and welded individuals into communities. But they are slowly giving up most of those roles; instead they have come to mean crime, decay, pollution and unrest.

No single reason will "explain" the complex difficulties that have engulfed many cities and perhaps threaten them all. But one fact stands out: Hand in hand, as these problems have intensified, open space has disappeared. (18 clauses, 29 active verbs, 132 words.)

120

CHAPTER 12

Off-Balance Sentences

Here are some quotations that never became famous:

To be, or not being, that is the question. --Shakespeare*

I came, I saw, and conquest took place. --Caesar**

You can fool some of the people all of the time, and all of the people some of the time; but it is darned near impossible for everyone to be fooled by you always. --Lincoln***

Even though off-balance sentences are among the most common writing flaws, your editor is likely to catch only the most obvious ones.   The rest slide by easily. Here are some sentences each of which, one way or another, lacks symmetry:

1. A person with high integrity either ought not run for political office or he should expect a lot of pressures for him to compromise.

2. Grady's work is as good or better than mine. He has not only improved his quality but he has increased his output. Compared to last year, his work has shown amazing improvement. Someone has either motivated him or he has gone on a better diet. He both has amazed me and astounded his boss.

3. Fendall either has not decided or can not, I'm not sure which.

The balanced versions are (corrected and related portions bold-faced):

1. A person with high integrity **either ought not** run for political office **or ought to** expect a lot of pressures for him to compromise.

2. Grady's work is **as good as or better than** mine. He has **not only** improved his quality **but also** increased his output. **Compared to his work last year, this year's work** has shown amazing improvement. **Either someone** has motivated him **or he** has gone on a better diet. He has **both amazed** me **and astounded** his boss.

3. Fendall **either has not decided** or **can not decide**, I'm not sure which.

---

* Crowell J. Shakespeare, Parsippany, NJ

** (Miss) Lura Belle Caesar, Morgue, AK

*** Joe Bob Lincoln, Parchicokey, LA

There are three categories of sentence imbalance. One is lack of parallelism. One is incomplete comparison. One is double-duty words. The most common is lack of parallelism--awkward series.

I. TALKING SENSE ABOUT PARALLEL STRUCTURE

Unlike some usage "faults," lack of parallelism is rarely a matter of right and wrong.

It is wrong to say, "I don't got any money." It is wrong to spell christmas without a capital letter. It is wrong to write, *I will go there yesterday*.

But who is to say at what point lack of parallelism is "wrong"? Here is a parallel sentence (parts of speech parenthesized).

> He liked hiking (*gerund*) and singing (*gerund*).

This one is not parallel:

> He liked hiking (*gerund*) and to sing (*infinitive*).

Well, it's pretty awkward, all right. That awkwardness gets disguised a bit when the sentence gets longer:

> (*Parallel*) He liked hiking/ in the mountains (*gerund, prepositional phrase*) and singing/ around the campfire (*gerund, prep. phrase*).
> (*Unparallel*) He liked hiking/ in the mountains (*gerund, prep. phrase*) and to sing /around the campfire (*infinitive, prep. phrase*).

That is still awkward, and a good writer would avoid writing it. But the next sentence has no awkwardness, even though it is non-parallel:

> He liked singing/ around the campfire (*gerund, prep. phrase*) and the joy /of outdoor life (*noun, prep. phrase*).

And this nonparallel example reads very nicely:

> He liked singing/ around the campfire (*gerund, prep. phrase*) and the joy/ it always brought him (*noun, dependent clause*).

Is that last readable example "wrong" because it is non-parallel? Only the ultimate fuss-budget (henceforth UFB) would mark you down for that. In fact, only a sharp-eyed grammarian (henceforth SEG) would be able even to detect it.

The point is: Non-parallelism can range from obvious to almost invisible. Sometimes it causes clumsy writing. Often it doesn't. You can get by with it.

Yet parallelism is a very important concept and the greatest structural tool you have for building sentences that are free of errors.

(And parallelism is also the basis of beautiful writing. Lincoln's Gettysburg Address, for instance, gains its emotional power and almost lyrical beauty from parallelism in both its small and its large elements. I recommend that you re-read it--often.)

The idea of parallelism is simple enough: that ideas or words sharing the same role in a sentence--subject, object, modifier--are best expressed in the same grammatical elements, and in the same pattern or order.

of the people, by the people, for the people. (*three prepositional phrases*)

Either he goes or I go. (*pronoun-verb, pronoun-verb*)

Wilson was scholarly, intellectual and questioning. (*three adjectives*)

These would be nonparallel:

Wilson was scholarly, intellectual and a questioning person. (*adjective, adjective and noun*)

He recommended that we add to the Tech Center, that we remodel the cafeteria and that the adjacent grounds should be re-landscaped. (*active-verb clause, active-verb clause, passive-verb clause.*)

NOW, ABOUT THOSE FRAGMENTS:

Teachers fret and stew over sentence fragments. But, as we noted earlier, fragmented sentences (a) don't occur often; (b) are generally deliberate, and (c) are likely to be useful. But fragments within a series--that's something else again. Series fragments (a) frequently occur; (b) are almost always careless and unintentional, and (c) cause clumsy and sometimes confusing writing.

Among the **advantages of the proposed chemical paint are that:**

1. It is environment-friendly, easy to dispose of in a biodegradable way.
2. **Manufacturability in large volume and at low cost.**
3. Competitors have not yet entered the field.

Above, you have two sentences and one fragment--a phrase. Number 2, which does not connect with the introduction, should be corrected to read:

2. **It is manufacturable** in large volume and at low cost.

Sequential items in a sentence should be parallel if possible.

> (*Non-parallel*) He found the play to be <u>amusing, touching, and a delight for all ages</u>. (*two adjectives, noun*)

> (*Made parallel*) He found the play to be <u>amusing, touching, and delightful</u> for all ages. (*three adjectives*)

Or you might rewrite to end the parallelism after the second item:

> He found the play to be amusing and touching--and a delight for all ages.

Important: The idea of parallelism is of much more value to you as a construction tool than it is as an error-catcher.

There are two common causes of unbalanced writing:

1. When a sentence gets long and the lack of parallelism is a matter of only a word or a transposition, the writer may find the problem hard to detect.

> (*Unparallel*) We will <u>either</u> **have to revise** the Technical Center budget estimate upward <u>or</u> **we will have to drop** some of the architectural frills.

> (*Balanced*) We will <u>either</u> **have to revise** the Technical Center budget estimate upward <u>or</u> **have to drop** some of the architectural frills.

2. In writing a list or series, the writer may forget that any words leading into it must also smoothly lead into *each of its elements individually*. Those words will apply to every item in the series until you call them off.

> He wore a plastic slicker, shirt, pants and muffler.

Call off that word *plastic* somehow, unless he truly had a complete plastic get-up.

> He wore a plastic slicker, plus shirt, pants, and muffler.
> He wore shirt, pants, muffler, and a plastic slicker.

This example also misfires:

> The team was eager, well trained, and had an excellent coach.

Reading into each series item individually:

> The team was/ eager
> The team was/ well trained
> **The team was/ had an excellent coach** OOPS!

For a balanced version, you might write:

> The team was eager, well trained and well coached.
> The team was eager and well trained, and had an excellent coach.

Sometimes, though, a parallel version sounds contrived or has less pizzazz than the original non-parallel sentence:

> This computer offers all the benefits of a traditional PC, the low price of a laptop and is bound to make you more efficient.

That is nonparallel, as this breakdown shows:

> This computer offers/ the benefits of a traditional PC,
> This computer offers/ the low price of a laptop and
> **This computer offers/ is bound to make you more efficient.**
> OOPS!

Here you would have to grunt and wheeze to stuff it into a contrived parallel format:

> This computer offers all the benefits of a traditional PC, the low price of a laptop and...
> greater personal efficiency for you? (*Nahhh!*)
> a guarantee that you will be more efficient? (*Nahhh!*)
> a way for you to become more efficient? (*Nahhh!*)

Rather than connive to make it parallel, it's best--as it often is--to use a Workaround, and recast the whole idea:

> This computer combines all the benefits of a traditional PC with the low price of a laptop. It is bound to make you more efficient.

Parallelism affects two elements of your writing: *Pairs of items,* combined, compared or contrasted; and *series of items or statements.*

> (*Nonparallel*) He is neither smart nor is he rich.
> (*Balanced*) He is neither smart nor rich.

> (*Nonparallel*) The food is sweet, tasty, and has lots of vitamins.
> (*Balanced*) The food is sweet, tasty, and full of vitamins.

When series are embodied in sentences, and the introductory words fit only some of the items, you have several possible solutions:

Typical aftermaths of a warm winter include a shortage of water, lawn chemicals and insect infestations.

Typical aftermaths of a warm winter include water and lawn-chemical shortages, and insect infestations. (*Introductory* **shortage** *removed.*)

Daily ⬤Blab
SHORTAGE OF BUG INFESTATION FEARED

Typical aftermaths of a warm winter include a shortage of water and of lawn chemicals--and insect infestations. (*End parallel portion with first* **and** *linking the two shortages.*)

Typical aftermaths of a warm winter include insect infestations and shortages of both water and lawn chemicals. (*Rearrange items so* **shortages** *no longer applies to* **insect infestations**.)

Here are two useful guidelines to insure parallelism:

1. There are five paired conjunctions that, by tradition, need to be followed by parallel grammatical elements. It's worth your memorizing the word pairs:

> **Either...or** and **neither...nor**
> **Whether...or**
> **Both...and**
> **Not only...but also**

If it is helpful to you, underline each of these whenever you use it, then look quickly to see whether your following words are parallel.

> He couldn't tell <u>whether</u> **she** was playing dumb <u>or</u> **that** she was just naturally not too bright.
> He was <u>either</u> **very smar**t <u>or</u> **he** was awfully lucky.
> Gorbachev's reforms affected <u>both</u> **the fabric** of Russian society <u>and</u> **changed** the history of the world.

A glance shows you none of the above is parallel, and you can repair each as you go:

> He couldn't tell <u>whether</u> **she was** playing dumb <u>or</u> **she was** naturally not too bright.
> He was <u>either</u> **very smart** <u>or</u> **awfully lucky**.
> Gorbachev's reforms <u>both</u> **affected** the fabric of Russian society <u>and</u> **changed** the history of the world.

2. Engrave into your mind the idea that the words introducing a series must also read naturally into *each item in that series.* If you run into a snag in a complicated sentence, it may help you to lay it out diagrammatically, as we did earlier:

> They allow you to replace **an** engine/fuel pump/tire, whatever.

> They allow you to replace an/ engine
>   to replace an/ **fuel pump** OOPS!
>   to replace an/ **tire** OOPS!

And you can easily correct it:

They allow you to replace **the** engine/fuel pump/tire, whatever.

One more:

> Among the advantages of this program are that you can do it at home, at your own pace and are able to review it at any time.

Diagramming that one shows its imbalance:

> Among the advantages of this program are that
> you can do it/ at home,
> you can do it/ at your own pace and
> you can do it/ **are able to review it at any time** OOPS!

And your revision:

> Among the advantages of this program are that you can **do** it at home, **work** at your own pace and **review** it at any time.

But parallel thinking goes beyond sentence diagnostics, into sentence creation. It produces an effective use of pairs and series, and these (including pairs and series of ideas) are a very large part of your writing. As you learn to spot them, put them into balance --make them parallel--you will have taken another large step toward Straightforward Writing.

Page 134 contains some examples to make the point. None of the originals violates parallelism; it's just that each ignored the chance to make the ideas parallel.

So, to complete the Five Principles of Straightforward Writing:

STRAIGHTFORWARD WRITING:

- → IS DRIVEN BY CLAUSES

- → IS POWERED BY ACTIVE VERBS

- → MATCHES CONTENT EMPHASIS AND GRAMMATICAL EMPHASIS

- → USES NOUNS AND VERBS THAT AFFECT THE SENSES

AND

- → **EMPHASIZES PARALLEL OR BALANCED STRUCTURE**

Let's look at the other two types of off-balance writing:

II. INCOMPLETE COMPARISONS

Recall our discussion of dangling participles. An introductory phrase without a subject will latch onto the first likely subject it comes to. That is how incomplete comparisons arise.

Don't compare apples and oranges, everyone says. Still, writers try. Notice the apples and the oranges here:

> Compared with <u>Spain</u>, the <u>climate</u> in Idaho has more variety.
> *Apple=Spain   Orange=climate*
> (*Corrected*) Compared with <u>the climate of Spain,</u> <u>that of Idaho</u>
>   has more variety.
> (*Corrected*) Compared with <u>Spain,</u> <u>Idaho</u> has a more-varied climate.

> Unlike <u>Fritz,</u> his brother's <u>nose</u> was classic, Roman.
> *Apple=Fritz   Orange=nose*
> (*Corrected*) Unlike <u>Fritz's nose,</u> <u>his brother's</u> was classic, Roman.
> (*Corrected*) Unlike <u>Fritz, his brother</u> had a classic Roman nose.

> Just like <u>1982</u>, the <u>election</u> in 1984 came down to the last few votes.
> *Apple=1982   Orange=election*
> (*Corrected*) Just as <u>in 1982,</u> the election <u>in 1984</u> came down to the
>   last few votes.
> (*Corrected*) Just like <u>the 1982 election,</u> <u>that of 1984</u> came down to
>   the last few votes.

Another common, if harmless, kind of incomplete comparison is:

> She is smarter than anyone in her class. (*Not true, unless she is smarter*
>   *than herself.*)
> (*Corrected*) She is smarter than anyone **else** in her class.
> (*But this is okay*) She is smarter than anyone in the other classes.

> There is no sound as good as popcorn popping.
> There is no **other** sound as good as popcorn popping.
> (*Okay*) There is no sound better than popcorn popping.

III. DOUBLE-DUTY VERBS

There are several ways a word may be called on to do double duty--do two jobs rather than one in a sentence. We're concerned here with verbs being called on for dual chores but being fit for only one.

You've learned that it serves the goal of conciseness not to repeat a word if you can comfortably avoid it.

We do not, will not, and should not stretch the Commission rules.

Very economical, saving two words:

> We do not [stretch], will not [stretch], and should not stretch the Commission rules.

But make sure that the omission doesn't cause grammatical confusion. Here the remaining verb helper tries, but fails, to do double duty--in this case, cover both past and present tenses:

> (*Off-balance*) Profits did not and never have reached the 1970 levels.
> (*Cross out the words* "and never have" *and you can see the problem.*)
> (*Balanced*) Profits did not **reach** and never have reached the 1970 levels.

When the above sentence order is changed, the error hides a bit better; but notice that it is still there:

> Profits did not reach the 1970 levels, and never have. (*Never have reach them?*)
> (*Balanced*) Profits did not reach the 1970 levels and never have **reached** them.

> (*Off-balance*) He **was** and continues to **star** in the film.
> (*Balanced*) He was **starring** and continues to star in the film.

> (*Off-balance*) For years he **has refused** the nomination, and he will continue to. (*To refused?*)
> (*Balanced*) For years he has refused the nomination, and he will continue to **refuse.**

And this total jumble--a verb trying to do *triple* duty:

> Although we **hadn't** previously, we now **do** and **will be going** to church regularly.

What one verb would fit all the lead-ins? Which *two?* It takes three.

> **[gone]**
> Although we hadn't done so previously, we now **go** to church--and **will be going** regularly.

The moral: Before you choose to knock out a word, make sure it's not propping up your sentence structure.

(When reviewing the examples on page 134 note, in addition to the clarifying power of parallelism, others of its beneficial byproducts: Shorter sentences, fewer words--but more clauses, more active verbs.)

HOW TO BE A REALLY ROTTEN EDITOR: (1) Always edit in red; (2) Always mark up the original, never a copy; (3) Use proper terms: Your rewording should always be referred to as "right" and your revisions as "corrections." (4) Edit only when in a bad mood; (5) Delay editing to the last minute. That puts your employee into the proper deadline-panic stage.

5: Straightforward Writing Emphasizes Parallel or Balanced Structure
SUMMARY AND APPLICATION NOTES

Summary:

Strong ideas, strongly positioned and grammatically emphasized, may gain further impact in yet another way: They can be arranged in parallel so the resulting sentence is balanced.

Parallelism means that ideas or words sharing the same job in a sentence are best expressed in the same grammatical elements and in the same syntax or "pattern."

Parallelism can be strictly followed. It can also be grossly violated. The former gives your writing dash, class, power, clarity. The latter makes you look clumsy.

But most writing falls between those extremes. It is neither unbalanced nor well balanced. It just fails to employ parallelism when it might have benefited by doing so.

Application Notes:

A newsmagazine, describing the aftermath of Hurricane Hugo, might have written this passage in this manner:

It was hard to find the neighborhood. Once you did, you would be lucky to find the street. And even if you managed to do that, individual houses were difficult to identify, being merely piles of boards and bricks. Nearby graffiti read LOOTERS WILL BE SHOT.

The real story gained by using parallelism (aided by the actual wording of the real-life graffiti). The underlinings are my own:

<u>Once you found</u> the neighborhood, <u>you had trouble</u> finding the street; <u>once you found</u> the street, <u>you had trouble</u> finding the house; <u>once you found</u> the house, all you saw was piles of boards and bricks. Nearby graffiti read <u>YOU LOOT, WE SHOOT.</u>

The example shows that parallelism is an artist's tool, to be employed with judgment. Here, the balance was carried on almost to the last, when the writer--for emphasis--chose to break from the parallel *"once you found...you had trouble"* wording.

Lincoln's *"of the people, by the people, for the people"* is perfectly parallel--three grammatically identical three-word prepositional phrases with a common object (*the people*). This example is perfectly parallel also:

At Crumherst, you will study; you will learn; you will succeed.

The next version also follows a pronoun/active verb parallelism:

In this classroom I will teach, you will study, and we both will learn.

The difference from the preceding version is slight: This one has three subjects (*I, you, we*) rather than one, and the final phrase adds one word (*both*). Yet no one but a Born-Again Fussbudget would criticize it as non-parallel. This next version *is* off-balance, however.

In this classroom I will be the teacher, you will study and learning will be a shared experience. (Pronoun/status verb/completer; pronoun/active verb; gerund/status verb/completer--a grammatical gumbo.)

The point is that any sentence is either *more* or *less* parallel. The better you can balance its elements, the stronger your writing will be. At the very least, try to avoid obvious lumpiness.

An easy place to bungle parallelism is in bulleted items. Magazine ads are common offenders; witness the apples and oranges in the left-hand version. Parallel revision is on the right.

THIS TRAVELING OFFICE:	*THIS TRAVELING OFFICE:*
. Holds 120 projects.	*. Holds 120 projects.*
. Includes pen holder and tablet.	*. Includes pen holder and tablet.*
. Built-in calculator.	*. Has a calculator built in.*
. Your initials are imprinted on cover.	*. Contains your initials on cover.*
. Available in black or brown.	*. Comes in black or brown.*

Notice on the left that only the first two bullets flow from the lead-in headline. The third is merely a label. The fourth is a stand-alone sentence. The fifth describes a characteristic of the product. Beginning each bullet with an active verb (right) solves the problem.

Learn to "think parallel." Watch for logically similar portions of your sentence, then try to fit them into balanced series and pairs. Look for common actions, common subjects,...common anything.

❋ Common actions.

You can avoid nuisance, avoid high costs and avoid traffic jams.

❋ Common subjects.

He swung, he missed, he swore under his breath.

❋ Common results.

Our refurbished aircraft fleet provides added space for the flight crew, more comfort for passengers and greater profitability for Lucky Airlines.

The next page shows the effect of balanced writing in three examples. In addition to making it easier on the reader, parallel thinking will also help you get your own ideas in order as you write.

THE POWER OF PARALLELISM

I

PARALLELISM NOT USED:
The migrants were united by many common problems, including the fact that they spoke English poorly, reflecting an education usually ending after third grade. The only jobs for which most of them were qualified were in seasonal agriculture, and coolness if not hostility was typical of the state's attitude toward migrants.
51 words, five clauses, one active verb

IMPROVED BY PARALLELISM:
The migrants were united by many common problems: Their English was poor; their education had usually ended by third grade; their jobs were mostly seasonal farm work; and their reception in the state ranged from cool to outright hostile.
39 words, five clauses, three active verbs

II

PARALLELISM NOT USED:
Writing sentences is difficult for a student unable to read sentences. The ability to learn almost any subject is difficult for the student lacking reading skills and, as a consequence, little work other than in menial laboring jobs will be available when he or she becomes an adult.
51 words, four clauses, one active verb

IMPROVED BY PARALLELISM:
Students who can't read sentences have trouble writing sentences; kids who can't write sentences have trouble learning just about anything. Young people who can't learn have trouble finding work outside of menial laboring jobs.
38 words, six clauses, nine active verbs

III

PARALLELISM NOT USED:
Broadbalk Field's acreage is divided into halves, each such section consisting of three strips subjected to different management. One strip is dressed heavily with barnyard manure. Chemical fertilizers are applied to the second strip, while the third one is left entirely untreated. Consistent results over 100 years show no difference in production between the chemically and the naturally fertilized fields; they both have rich yields, in the same amounts. But the unfertilized acreage produces poorly, about one-fiftieth of the other strips.
83 words, seven clauses, four active verbs

IMPROVED BY PARALLELISM:
Broadbalk Field's acreage is split into two sections. Each section is divided into three strips. The first absorbs a heavy dressing of barnyard manure; the second receives a treatment of chemical fertilizers; the third gets no help at all. For a hundred years the results have been the same: the "naturally" fertilized field and the chemically fertilized acres yield richly, and in the same amount. The unfertilized acreage produces poorly, one-fiftieth of the other strips.
75 words, eight clauses, five active verbs

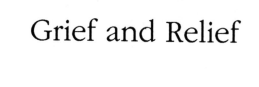

Grief and Relief

CHAPTER 13

The Five Big Ones

Asked to guess the worst grammar problems, most people would guess wrong.

There are five big ones. It's possible that they are not the ones your editor pounces on. Three of them relate to wordiness; the fourth and probably the fifth, to lack of care.

This example contains all five of them:

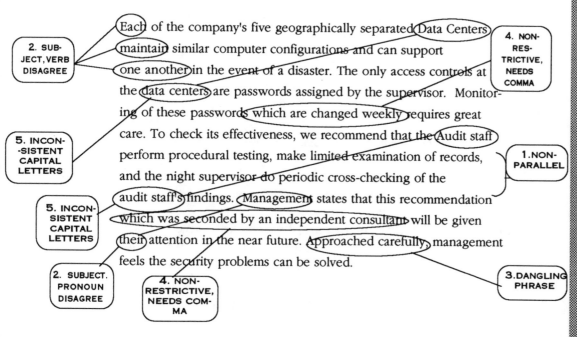

The five are:

1. The "A,B,3" sequence. In other words, parallel ideas are not using parallel language. The faulty portion above reads:

>..we recommend that the Audit staff:
>>**perform** procedural testing,
>>**make** limited examination of records and
>>**the night supervisor do** periodic cross-checking
>>of the audit staff's findings.

Made parallel, it would read:

>...we recommend **that the Audit staff perform** procedural testing **and make** limited examination of records, **and that the night supervisor do** periodic cross-checking of the Audit staff's findings.

Because chapter 12, Off-Balance Sentences, dealt thoroughly with parallelism as a principle of Straightforward Writing, no more will be said about the matter here. Just remember: When you deal with ideas in pairs or in series, they are much clearer to read if they line up grammatically.

2. Subject-verb (and noun-pronoun) squabbles. Two manifestations of this problem show up in the first sentence:

> **Each** of the company's five geographically separated Data Centers **maintain** similar computer configurations and can **support one another** in the event of a disaster.

Corrected, the sentence would read:

> **Each** of the company's five geographically separated Data Centers **maintains** similar computer configurations and can support **the others** in the event of a disaster. (*Note that **the others** excludes **each**; in the original, **one another** included **each**.*)

A second example:

> **Management states** that this recommendation...will be given **their** attention.
> (*Corrected*) **Management states** that this recommendation...will be given **its** attention. (*Or,* that **it** will give this recommendation....)

3. Misplaced modifying clauses and phrases (restrictive vs. non-restrictive). The example contains a participial phrase--not dangling but, worse, attaching to the wrong noun:

> Approached carefully, management feels the security problems can be solved.

Unless the writer truly meant sneaking up on management, the correct version would attach the modifier to its proper noun:

> Approached carefully, the security problems can be solved, management feels.

4. Punctuation inconsistency in modifying clauses. A clause that defines (or for that matter, a phrase that defines) should not be set apart with commas. One that merely comments should be. These are incorrect:

> Monitoring of these passwords which are changed weekly requires great care.
> Management feels that this recommendation which was seconded by an independent consultant will be given...

In each case the modifying clause provides comment, not definition:

> Monitoring of these passwords which are changed weekly
> requires great care.
> *(The passwords already were defined in the preceding sentence, and are referred to as* <u>these passwords</u>. *The clause* which are changed weekly *merely adds information; the sentence would be clear without it.)*

> *(Corrected)* Monitoring of these passwords, which are changed weekly, requires great care.

Similarly:

> *(Incorrect)* Management feels that this recommendation which
> was seconded by an independent consultant will be given...

> *(Corrected)* Management feels that this recommendation,
> which was seconded by an independent consultant, will be given...

5. Inconsistent style. The two pairs that don't jibe in the example both have to do with capitalization:

> Data Centers *(line 1) and* data centers *(line 4).*

> the Audit staff *(line 6) and* the audit staff's findings *(line 9).*

Taking these problems in order:

⇥ SUBJECT-VERB SQUABBLES

Unlike a lot of grammar rules, which are purely matters of preference, this one does deal with right and wrong. A singular subject has to have a singular verb, a plural subject a plural verb.

Now, you knew that without my telling you. You would not write, for instance:

> My boss are the best manager in this company.

> His research show that we is losing market share.

> Seventy-six trombones makes a lot of noise or music, as
> the case may be.

Yet subject-verb disagreements, as grammarians call them, are very likely the single most common writing problem.

A sampler of incorrect examples:

> Once the first **pass** at the MAS Document and Database **are** complete...

> As more **detail and information is** determined about the component...

> **Statements** of Additional Information about the fund and its performance over the past year **is** enclosed.

> **Everyone** aged 50 and over and employed more than 25 years **are** eligible for early retirement.

This problem seems, if anything, to be getting worse. (And, interestingly, it occurs almost equally often in the writing of poorly and well-educated people.) So I've tried to analyze its causes and--without anything so formal as a crusade--set out to provide a possible cure for this number one grief-producer.

Those causes, it seems to me, are some combination of the following:

- Sentences get too long; too many words intrude between subject and verb.

- The writer, while working through a sentence, reads back only as far as the nearest noun.

- The previous sentence has already set up a singular-plural relationship, which the writer then forgets.

- Any adjoining noun and verb look like they belong together.

- Certain nouns or pronouns may be either singular or plural; some others are plural in form but grammatically singular. They sometimes cause confusion.

- The writer overlooks the power of *and* to create plural subjects and *or* to create singular ones.

☞ Sentences get too long.

If the subject snuggles right against the verb, no one but a near-illiterate will mix singular and plural. But if 1000 words should intervene (and, no, I suppose this has never happened), the chance of a singular-plural mixup would be pretty close to 50-50.

The more words in the sentence, the more nouns and pronouns pop up between subject and verb. Any one of them may distract the writer (these "false subjects" are underlined in this passage:)

> All orders received by a <u>fund</u> other than the <u>Market Fund</u> and the <u>Government Bond Fund</u> and approved by our review <u>committee</u> or any <u>member</u> is considered valid. (***orders...are*** *considered valid.*)

☞ <u>The writer doesn't look far enough back in the sentence to find the real subject.</u>

Given the number of would-be subjects in a long sentence, it is important (see chapter 3) that you re-read each sentence *in full* before you continue. Especially since

☞ <u>Any adjoining noun and verb **look** like they belong together.</u>

> All orders received by a <u>fund</u> other than the <u>Market Fund</u> and the <u>Government Bond Fund</u> and approved by our review <u>committee</u> or any <u>member is</u> considered valid.

If the word *member* doesn't compel the writer to use the singular *is*, the next noun back, *committee*, may; or the next; or....

So, burn deeply into your mind something you already know: Noun-verb proximity may mean nothing at all. It's like two people huddled under an awning in the rain; they may or may not be closely acquainted.

While you're searching back to find the subject, might as well re-read the previous sentence also. That can help you avoid the next problem:

☞ <u>The preceding sentence may have already decided the singular-or-plural question.</u>

> Make sure that PITCH, WIDTH and SPACE **are** the same in either configuration. If it **is** not, then I recommend...

✏ <u>Certain nouns and pronouns can be either singular or plural, depending on what you intend them to mean. And some pronouns that look plural are considered singular grammatically.</u>

First category first:

Nouns representing groups (*team, management, committee, faculty...*) may be used as plurals if you intend them to mean the members of the group. If you intend them to mean the group as a unit,

"If a book can be called a 'good read,' then a restaurant can be a 'good eat'; a plane can be a 'good fly'; a play, a 'good sit'; and a funeral, a 'good bury.'"

--Martin Willsted

> **GRAMMATICALLY SPEAKING**
>
> A noun representing a group is called a **collective noun.**

they take singular verbs--and pronouns. So each of these examples is correct:

> The team **like** to tell **their** favorite off-color water-polo stories. *(Each member has a joke.)*
> The team often **sneaks** off to **its** favorite restaurant for quiche. *(They all like the place.)*

The most likely problem is that you may mix them:

> *(Incorrect)* The faculty **has voted** for **their** favorite candidates and then adjourned **its** meeting.
> *(Acceptable)* The faculty have voted for their favorite candidates and then adjourned their meeting.
> *(Or, using a Workaround)* The faculty has adjourned its meeting after the members voted for their favorite candidates.

A related fact: Some pronouns that seem to be plural are considered grammatically singular. You may wish to memorize them. On the other hand, in conversation you already use them right.

Those words include *everyone, anyone, anybody, nobody,* and *each.* You might ask in conversation, "Is everybody happy?" yet write:

> *(Incorrect)* Everybody present at the anniversary dinner were given gifts.
> *(Correct)* Everybody present at the anniversary dinner **was given a gift.**
> *(Notice that **gift** also has to be singular.)*

Sometimes those words can give you fits. How do you handle these, for instance?

> Everyone blew their noses/his nose/his or her nose.
> Nobody was/were hurt, was/were they?

Almost any version of either one sounds contrived:

> Everyone blew their noses. *(Grammatically wrong.)*
> Everyone blew their nose. *(They owned one collectively?)*
> Everyone blew his or her nose. *(Right, but silly.)*
> Everyone blew his nose. *(Right, but sexist.)*
>
> Nobody was hurt, was they?
> Nobody were hurt, were they?
> Nobody was hurt, were they? *(Mixing of singular and plural.)*

Those are classic instances calling for a Workaround:

> They all blew their noses.
> Nobody was hurt, isn't that so?

Some pronouns, including *some, all, more, most* and *any* take a singular verb if they represent something singular, a plural verb if they represent something plural. You'll have no trouble with them:

"Some of my mush (*singular*) is missing!" bawled Baby Bear.
Some of these procedures (*plural*) were apparently written by the boss's
  son or a comparable college-trained nitwit.

Some plural words are singular in meaning and take singular verbs. Most of them won't fool you; some correct examples:

The news was (*not* were) discouraging today.
Measles is (*not* are) a childhood disease.
Rhyhm and blues was (*not* were) her favorite music.
Ten minutes is (*not* are) too long to listen to the "Minute Waltz"
  on the bagpipe.

☞ The writer forgets the power of *and* to make a subject plural or
  nor and *or* to make a subject singular.

An *and* turns the subject plural--but only *and*; other connectors do not, such as *together with, rather than, including* and *as well as*. So both these versions are correct:

His **life and his work were** depicted on television.
His **life**, along with his work, **was** depicted on television.

An exception: A singular modifier makes a compound subject take a singular verb:

Every cat and dog requires (*not* require) love and care.

Nor and *or* do not link; they separate. They call for singular verbs.

(*Incorrect*) Neither Fendall nor Mrs. Carson are interested in Bach.
(*Fendall* **is** *not interested nor* **is** *Mrs. Carson interested; therefore.*)
Neither Fendall nor Mrs. Carson **is** interested in Bach.

When half the subject is plural and the other half singular (*the woman or her children*), there is no "right" answer. The tidiest solution is to put the plural second followed by a plural verb:

Neither the woman nor her **children are** able to read.

VERB ODDS AND ENDS:

❋ If you create an inverted sentence order, it may help you to think of it in standard subject/verb/completer sequence first. It is easier to choose your verb then.

142

(*Inverted*) Also interesting to Chinatown visitors was/were the rickshaw rental and the Wok Around the Clock 24-hour restaurant.

(*Put into standard sequence*) The rickshaw **rental and** the Wok Around the Clock 24-hour **restaurant were** also interesting to Chinatown visitors.

✱ If it links a singular subject and plural completer, or vice versa, a status verb (*is, are*, etc.) agrees with the subject--even if you invert the sentence. So both of these are correct:

His big **problem is** his small ears.
His small **ears are** his big problem.

✱ The pronouns *who, that,* and *which* are either singular or plural depending on what noun they replace.

Watching the violinist reminds me of Grampaw (*singular*), who always fiddles with his beard.

The sauna brought to mind Finnish peasants (*plural*), who roll in the snow after steam-bathing and whop each other with hazel switches.

As noted in Chapter 6, it's wise to select these pronouns carefully so they don't refer to an unintended noun.

He showed me drawings of instruments that were very poorly produced. (*That is, poorly produced instruments?*)

He showed me drawings of instruments that were very poorly produced. (*Somebody made some poor copies?*)

➥ "DANGLERS" AND ORPHANS

Make up some next words to follow these sentence beginnings. Go ahead; I'll wait while you do:

1. Blinded by the bright footlights,_____. . .

2. Discovered by Spanish explorers in the 12th century, _____. . .

3. A product of US automotive expertise, _____ . . .

I don't know your exact sentence, of course. But you probably thought of something like the following:

1. Blinded by the bright footlights, the actor (or perhaps **the audience)....**

2. Discovered by Spanish explorers in the 12th century, the island (or some geographic feature)......

The REASON for the recent memo sent to you regarding the CHANGES to the operating PROCEDURES....

...WERE!
ah-hah-hah-hah!

SUBJECT-VERB DISAGREEMENTS are the most common writing problem. Like many others, they occur far more often when sentences are long and the verbs are weak.

3. A product of US automotive expertise. the new Hotshot 6 (or
   other vehicle)....

At any rate, you certainly did not write anything like these
sentences:

1. Blinded by the bright footlights, the script...
   Blinded by the bright footlights, the script couldn't be read by the actors.

2. Discovered by Spanish explorers in the 12th century, fishing....
   Discovered by Spanish explorers in the 12th century, fishing is the
   island's main occupation.

3. A product of US automotive expertise, the price.....
   A product of US automotive expertise, the price of the new
   Hotshot 6 is a surprise.

Had you done that, you would have created "dangling" phrases.
The fact that you didn't, shows that no one has to tell you not to use
dangling participles. You already know that. However, it's easy to
become careless and forget that

 A phrase with no subject of its own (but a mind of its own) will adopt
the closest noun or pronoun.

Like *split infinitive*, the term *dangling participle* has become a
catchword for all grammatical errors. However, unlike a split infinitive, which is harmless and often useful, the dangling participle can
distort the meaning of what you write.

Usually it won't. Much of the time it won't be noticed, and your
meaning will come through. No harm done there. At other times
people will see your goof and chuckle. Again, no harm; we all can
use a good laugh now and again.

But there are those times when--like any grammar error--the dangler will create a meaning you don't intend.

The DP is typical of all misplaced modifying phrases and clauses.
The true dangler (which is actually not very common) lives up to its
name: It does begin with a participle, and it does dangle--hang at
one end of a sentence that omits its subject entirely.

Mean-tempered and surly, his lips curled with hatred. (*Surly lips?*)

The necessary pronoun *he* is absent. In most cases, however, the
subject is there all right, but it is separated from the modifying
phrase--which conveniently latches onto another subject instead.

145

Since any kind of phrase (or any single-word modifier, for that matter) can dangle, why is the "dangling participle" so often singled out? I believe it is because of its semi-verb content, suggesting action: *Running, thinking, hitting* (present participles) or *rejected, discouraged, connected* (past participles). A strong magnetism draws such action words toward the nearest likely (or even unlikely) actors:

> Standing as tall as five men, the brain of the dinosaur was nothing to brag about.
> Squatting in the shadows of the Sierras, your reporter finally located the town of Redbow.
> Intending to fly to New York, his travel schedule was revised.

Don't blush if your modifiers dangle. You're in good company. Here are some from the work of professional writers. (Notice that dangling can occur at either end of a sentence, or amidship.)

> (*From a Fortune 500 corporate annual report*) The company's library is large for its size.
> (*In a professional ad for dental implants*) Once in place, your natural jawbone bonds to the implant...
> (*And in the same ad*) They usually let you eat anything you want, like natural teeth.
> (*From a biography of Washington*) Sixty-one years old, his waist was only 35.
> (*From a best-selling cookbook*) Similar to tomato Florentine, opinions are mixed on salmon dill.
> (*From TV's "60 Minutes"*) They left the castle where the much-publicized bombing took place three minutes ahead of the explosion.
> (*From Red Cross instruction book on resuscitation*) Remove your mouth, listening for outflow of air.

And here are three all from the same source--the movie synopses from the in-flight magazine of my favorite airline:

> Set in the thriving aviation community of Los Angeles in 1938, daring pilot Cliff Secord finds...
> Left with amnesia and intense flashbacks, his wife and friends paint contrasting pictures of his past.
> In assisting his father to become self-sufficient again, the two men grow closer together.

Single-word and clause modifiers may dangle, too, but that is less common. Words usually fall naturally into the appropriate slots. And clauses have the protection of containing both the subject and the verb. However, if a clause includes a pronoun, be careful to make it clear which noun it represents.

Pronouns are prankish little fellers, ever likely to hook onto some word you hadn't intended.

> After they had killed 14 persons, the doctors isolated the responsible viruses.
> Although it runs from Ontario to the Rockies, the fox finds its range increasingly controlled by ranchers.

Don't infer that all, or even most, misplaced modifiers are comic knee-slappers. They are not. Some do produce humor; others, confusion. You certainly don't want your reader to be confused; whether you want him or her to snicker at you is your own choice.

It is really hard to overstate the importance of the principle: Keep related elements together.

➪ DEFINITIONS VS. COMMENTS

Modifier clauses--and, to a lesser degree, modifier phrases--do one of two things: They either *define* or identify whatever they modify; or they *comment* on something whose identity is already known by the reader.

It's important that you be clear as to which job your modifier is doing--and that you signal that function to your reader. The most useful signal is correct punctuation.

If the modifier defines or identifies, it should be integral with the sentence, not set off by punctuation marks. If it comments on an already defined element, it must be set off by punctuation, typically commas.

> **GRAMMATICALLY SPEAKING**
>
> A clause or phrase that defines an element is said to be **restrictive**--restricting that element's meaning. One that merely adds information is called **non-restrictive**; the information added is not essential to the sentence's meaning.

As noted elsewhere, memory gimmicks usually don't work--except for those you make up yourself. That having been said, here is an easy way to keep your punctuation straight:

If the modifier **comm**ents, it requires **comm**as.

(Well--I like it.)

Each usage problem in this chapter is included for a different reason. Subject-verb disagreements are the most common problem; danglers, the most embarrassing one.

Confusion over defining vs. commenting modifiers is included

Figures of speech should be imaginative. But not too imaginative. Mixing two images, for instance, often results in a half-breed that makes no sense. Here is a collection, all from one company:

His ears lit up.

He's burning the midnight oil at both ends.

They should kiss the feet you walk on.

We can't count our sheep before they hatch.

He really bit the farm.

I know it like the back of my mind.

He doesn't want to be a guinea pigeon.

I'm not going to bite off my nose to spite my face.

Let's meet them halfway a little bit.

He's a one-man shop that operates out of the seat of his pants.

We're just reading behind the lines.

Let's not beleaguer the point.

It's on the tip of my mind

We don't want to rub that in their nose.

--Compiled by Nikki Johnston

because it is the error most likely to cause clouded, unclear writing.

Here are some clauses, each one used both in defining (D) and commenting (C) ways:

C. Cheapskate restaurateur O.K Grubb, <u>who has grown</u> <u>tired of paying to launder dirty table linen</u>, now uses paper tablecloths and cleans them with artgum erasers.

(Cheapskate restaurateur O.K. Grubb now uses paper tablecloths and cleans them with artgum erasers *is correctly understood without the modifying clause, which merely adds comment.*)

D. Anyone <u>who has grown tired of paying to launder dirty table linen</u> could just try dimming the house lights.

(Anyone could just try dimming the house lights *makes little sense without the modifying clause defining it.*)

D. The woman <u>who is standing under the marquee</u> is not really Bubbles LaTour. (*Clause defines which woman is meant.*)

C. My nearsighted mother, <u>who is standing under the marquee</u>, is really the former Bubbles LaTour. (*Ma is already identified.*)

C. All pet iguanas, <u>which are too scaly to be really fun</u>, ought to be kept out of the kitchen. (*Keep all iguanas out.*)

D. All pet iguanas <u>which are too scaly to be really fun</u> ought to be kept out of the kitchen. (*Let the fuzzier ones in.*)

C. I saw him Wednesday, <u>before his trial for calling a Hare Krishna "Baldy."</u> (*His trial occurred after Wednesday.*)

D. I saw him Wednesday <u>before his trial for calling a Hare Krishna "Baldy."</u> (*His trial was Wednesday; I saw him earlier that day.*)

Phrases, like clauses, also either offer comment (C) or provide definition (D). The same punctuation guidelines apply.

C. Joe Dimbulb, <u>fed up with folks saying "Hi, Joe, whaddya know?",</u> had his name changed to Preston Dimbulb.

D. People <u>fed up with folks saying "Hi, Joe, whaddya know?"</u> should answer by quoting large sections of the encyclopedia.

C. Luciano the Yodeling Dog Tenor, <u>expecting wild applause,</u> lost the Broadway part because he couldn't tapdance.

D. Any jazz singer <u>expecting wild applause</u> should not perform at prayer meetings or funerals.

148

Get the idea? Good. Now give these next examples a try. Mark each as defining or commenting, and insert commas where they belong. (Not all of them are easy calls.)

1. He introduced us to his mother <u>Martha.</u>
2. Alexander Fleming <u>who discovered penicillin</u> was a hero to many ill people.
3. The man <u>who discovered penicillin</u> was Alexander Fleming,
4. Willie <u>who is always efficient</u> finished the duet a minute ahead of his plodding sister.
5. An employee <u>who is always efficient</u> is a rare bird.
6. The old building <u>condemned in 1949</u> is still standing--or possibly leaning against the one next door.

Your answers should read:

1. Commenting; comma needed. He has only one mother.
2. Commenting. Fleming is already identified. Commas needed.
3. Defining, no commas.
4. Commenting, commas. Sentence is clear without these words.
5. Defining, no commas.
6. We have no way of knowing.

To make a decision on number 6, you would have to know the context. If the preceding sentences have identified the building, the modifying phrase merely adds comment. If no identifying has been done, the phrase identifies what building is being talked about.

I should note that in casual usage you don't need to get too fussy about the point in number 1. These, although possibly incorrect, would pass muster:

Yeah--and so's your Aunt Minnie! (*Only a grammatical snob would make it:* So's your Aunt, Minnie!)
Let's go visit your Uncle Eddie. (*O.K. no matter how many uncles you have.*)
This is my old pal Johnny. (*O.K. even if he is your only pal in the whole world.*)

When you use clauses, you sometimes have another way to tip off your reader as to whether it is commenting or defining. That is, when the clause may begin with either *that* or *which*, choose *that* for defining clauses, *which* for commenting clauses.

That used to be a hard and fast rule--and one I happen to like. But it has been defied by enough good writers that it has lost the force it once had. It is still a sound practice. I recommend it.

ETC.

The ultimate lazy word, it probably will never die. Meaning "and other things of the same kind," it is used for all sorts of related and unrelated purposes, including finishing a sentence you don't know how to finish otherwise.

What does "letters, procedures, etc." mean? Manuals? Memos? Catalogs? Anything that is written?

How about "household animals: dogs, cats, etc."? What else is left? Possums?

Are there any "rules" for the use of *etc.*?

1. Use it seldom. Better yet, not at all. Its absence will make you think more clearly about what you are really saying.

2. Use it only in its true meaning, not as a substitute for "Oh, I could go on and on."

3. Avoid using it redundantly:

And etc.
etc. and so forth.
Such things as.....etc.

Etc.

Not only does it clearly signal which kind of clause modifier you have, it also is natural--very much a reflection of the way we speak. No one in conversation would say, for example, *Is this the hat which you wanted?* or *The job which I told you about.* The choice, when talking, is clearly *that.*

Writing guru Rudolf Flesch advocated ferreting out and replacing all unnecessary *whiches.* He called the process "which hunting"; I like that.

When you're in doubt whether a modifier is commenting or defining, here are two guidelines that may help:

✏ If the modifier would look right within parentheses, it is a commenter, and needs commas. This one meets that test:

> The lead baritone (who was very formal) sang "Am Not
> Misbehaving."
> (*So write*) The lead baritone, who was very formal, sang "Am Not
> Misbehaving."

This one flunks it:

> Anyone (who was very formal) would have been laughed out
> of the cowpokes' bunkhouse.
> (*So write*) Anyone who was very formal would have been laughed
> out of the cowpokes' bunkhouse.

✏ If the modifier and the element it modifies would work as well in two separate sentences, the phrase or clause is a commenter, and needs commas. This one works:

> The lead baritone sang "Am Not Misbehaving." He was very formal.

And this one does not:

> Anyone would have been laughed out of the cowpokes'
> bunkhouse. He was very formal.

➥ APPLES AND ORANGES; THE MATTER OF CONSISTENCY

In any piece of writing, this is the most predictable usage problem, and the one most likely to be detected. It doesn't take a language expert to notice if you write *I(a)*, then *2(B)*--or that you refer to *George Johnson* in one line and **Mr. Hiram Mork** in another, or refer to *Mr. Mork* in one paragraph and *Mork* in another. Any message contains hundreds of opportunities to mix apples and oranges.

This problem doesn't lend itself to specific suggestions for improvement, because the possible inconsistencies are so many. As a general precaution: If you find that, no matter how you stare, style inconsistencies hide from you, ask a friend, secretary or colleague to scrutinize your message for that problem only. Ideally, pick a Fussbudget for this task. Ask him or her to be really rough on you.

You are most likely to be consistent in things taught in school or required by your employer: These include letter or report format, double- or triple-spacing documents, block or indented paragraph style, margins, punctuation and capitalization.

You are least likely to be consistent in things that occur only now and then. A new name comes up, The Franklin Mint and Cotton Candy Co. The second time it appears you decide to refer to it as *Franklin Mint*. On the next page it occurs again; forgetting you already called it something else, you refer to it as *Franklin*. Further on, it may become *Franklin Co.*, and so on. It is understandably easy for this to happen.

No message is typical. But here is what an inconsistency-filled paragraph looks like.

Be sure GH has been run prior to Bobcat. If there are net length limits the .net file should be present. Bobcat will be run 1 time using placement files generated by Dapr. Refer to *Chapter 4, Partitioning.* If you edit the project file, I recommend you edit it two times for accuracy. If the CHOPR width is more than DAPR, it will widen the pin to dapr size. (Refer to chapter 5, *MAS Database.*) The major commands are GET (read) and PUT, or write, data. When getting (loading) setup data, the tools will follow a well-defined path. When asked if you want to store the set-up data answer yes and your data will be checked in; answer "No" and your data will be written to your file and remains locked.

Sign up that Fussbudget now. He or she can do you a great favor by pointing out those little inconsistencies that may otherwise blemish your final message.

..and Some Lesser Ones (Perhaps)

Are you ever annoyed by those grab-bag collections of this and that called Handy Hints, or Useful Tips? I am. They too often substitute sketchy, hit-and-miss information for thorough analysis--and imply simplistic solutions to complex problems. I don't intend that this chapter be such a collection, or be seen that way.

It deals with a dozen-plus writing issues, from nuisance-level to severe, as they have been expressed by participants in my workshops over the years. I present them here in the belief that these problems may be fairly general.

A lot of chronic difficulties are not here. I've tried to avoid rehashing, yet one more time, the oldies and goodies that you see in every grammar book (*uninterested/disinterested, compared to/compared with, data is vs. data are, different from/different than*...you know them). I've noted a few of these only when I felt able to present them in a new and useful light.

Affect, Effect

Almost as common as transposing these terms is seeing them in lists of Commonly Confused Words. The puzzle is, given all the publicity, why the problem should persist. But it does. Here is an unusual example in that it contains both misuses:

> In weighing the <u>affect</u> of the current budget cuts, we too seldom
> consider how they <u>effect</u> the poor and elderly.

To *affect* means to cause an *effect*. If that is hard to remember, try this: The cause precedes the effect--just as A (*affect*) comes before E (*effect*).

(Both words also have less-common uses--but you will rarely need them. Stick with getting these two straight.)

Ambiguous Little Words

In advising writers to be concise, the advisors too often forget to point out that small and simple words are more likely to be ambiguous than big ones are. Most large words have specific definitions; small ones have many, many possible meanings. Check the six-to-eight-column-inch dictionary definition lists for *that, for, as...*

Are headache pain and relief of headache pain the same thing? It would seem so:

Take these pills twice daily for headache pain.
Take these pills twice daily for relief of headache pain.

Hello. I'm calling for John Fleming. (*On behalf of John? Or trying to find John?*)
He had jimmied the window so it wouldn't open. (*Did he jimmy it for that purpose; or was it stuck shut because he accidentally jimmied it?*)
Fredericks drove home to find his kids playing with matches. (*Was that his purpose in driving home?*)

There is no profound advice here--just a reminder not to get cocky and figure it's easier to control little words just because they're little.

Apostrophe Ambiguity

The apostrophe does a couple of useful things: It shows possession and it designates an omission of a letter or letters. Sometimes it's hard to remember just which job it's doing. That can drive a poor speller nuts--especially with these words:

Their, there, they're, there's, theirs, your, you're, its, it's.

It clears the air to remember that a personal pronoun showing possession never has an apostrophe. Never. So that takes care of *their, theirs, its, your* and *yours.*

If the remaining contractions still cause trouble, I recommend using the full spelling until you become confident. Just thinking of them as two words helps:

they're, there's, you're, it's
(Use) they are, there is, you are, it is (*or* it has).

As

Used to designate cause or reason (*As you are the oldest one here, you deserve this*), *as* is a poor substitute for *since*. In turn, *since* is a poor substitute for *because.*

You'll never go wrong with *because*. But either of the others may cause ambiguity.

Since you have taken over the job...
(*Does this mean because? Or does it mean between that time and now?*)

As I have presented the matter to the Committee...
(*Does this mean because? Or does it refer to the way in which the matter was presented?*)

This doesn't mean to avoid those words. It does mean to be careful that they convey only one meaning.

A related vague substitute is *while* for *although*, as in:

154

> While he was a hard worker, he never earned enough to
>   keep his car in gasoline.
> (*During the time he worked hard? Or although he worked hard?*)

It ought not be used as a weak substitute for either an *and* or a semicolon:

> Georgiana French will serve as new president, while Carl Jonas is
>   representative to the national group.
> (*This suggests, falsely, that her term will last only during the time
>   he is the representative.*)

The safe use for *while* is to mean *during the time that*. Stick with that--and with *because* for most cause-and-effect sentences.

Complete

With all the fussing over *most unique,* I find it interesting that no one objects to *most complete*. If a shop has "a complete stock of imported wines," does that mean it will haul out, on request, a bottle of 1989 Galapagos Island Riesling? I doubt it. The shop may have an "almost complete" stock, but I doubt even that.

The point is, no one expects *complete* to mean complete--and no one cares a whole lot, either. And that's just how it will be with *unique* also--no matter how its detractors detract. Although I opt for its precise use, I do so knowing the cause is lost, and not worrying much about it. There are more important battles to fight.

But if we let *unique*'s meaning become diluted by overuse, wails one purist, what words can we use to mean one of a kind?

How about *one of a kind?*

Comprise

Here is an example of being too smart for your britches. If you write in an annual report, *The company comprises three divisions*, you can bet that the CEO, the corporate lawyer or someone in the Public Relations staff will correct it and write: *The company is comprised of three divisions*. Some will also favor you with a little pedagogic note to the effect that the divisions comprise the company, the company does not comprise the divisions. This has happened to me, often.

Hang in there. You (a shrinking minority) are right and they (the growing majority) are wrong. *Comprise* carries much of the meaning of *include*. So their correction won't play; a company can no more be comprised of divisions than it can be included of divisions.

The whole comprises its parts. The parts *constitute, make up* or *compose* the whole.

Then why not just use the simpler word *include* instead of *comprise*? Because they come close in meaning, but not close enough. A baseball team may **include** two Cubans, but it **comprises** nine people.☞

Now a question only you can answer: Since probably 80 per cent of your readers who have an opinion will think you have used *comprise* incorrectly, would you prefer to be right and thought wrong, or write it wrong and be judged right?

I have no recommendation on the matter.

Each
Although *each* is singular, it often bumps against a plural verb. Are these examples right or wrong?

> 1. Riordan and Johnson each were given a $5000 fine.
> 2. Each of them was given a $5000 fine.
> 3. They each are subject to further penalties.
> 4. They are each subject to a further penalty.

They are all correct, even though at first glance they look inconsistent. Here are the guidelines:

✏ The subject of the sentence governs the verb. Thus, in example 1: *Riordan and Johnson....were.* In example 2: *Each.....was.*

✏ Any later noun is singular or plural depending on whether *each* goes before or after the verb. If the *each* comes before the verb, the following noun (*penalties* in number 3) is plural. If *each* follows the verb, the noun (*penalty* in number 4) becomes singular.

Fighting Losing Battles
I don't advocate flouting sensible rules or flaunting their misuse (see Flout and Flaunt on the next page, if you want to). But language changes--faster than most editor's minds do. There is no sense railing at wrong usage that is past correction.

For example, there may be little point in trying to stop the "wrong" use of *hopefully*, as in *The task will be finished, hopefully by tomorrow.* The word seems not to have a substitute anyone likes, such as *it is to be hoped that.* Also, writers will continue to use *contact* as a verb no matter who says it is an improper coinage. And they will keep saying *enormity* to mean large size even though it really means wickedness.

☞ This suggests that when you write *include* you should be sure you don't mean *comprise.*

COMPLETE STOCK OF MEN'S SHIRTS
I'd like a blue short-sleeved shirt
we only got green in short sleeves
then I'll take light green
what we got is dark green
how about green long-sleeves?
long-sleeves don't come in green
would y'believe, a pair of sox?

This is really advice to editors: It's more productive to spend your time on things that may be changed. No sense beating a dead horse, to coin an old saying.

Flout, Flaunt

There is no great call on the job for you to use either of these words; but writers heed that call anyway, most often by using them wrong.

> We can not allow this one department to flaunt our policies.

A company could, if it wished, *flaunt* its policies--that is, make a showy display of them; but a rebellious department *flouts* them--makes a point of disobeying them.

Until using these correctly becomes second nature, you may rely on equally good substitutes: *show off* for *flaunt* and *scorn* for *flout*.

Imply, Infer

Another perpetual contender for most confused word pair. I think the problem is that many misusers believe they mean the same thing; and *infer* sounds the more "educated" of the two.

The more useful word to learn is *infer*, since it has no very good one-word synonym. It means to conclude by reasoning, from something assumed or known. *Deduce* comes close, but is not likely to be widely used.

Imply has workable substitutes. *Suggest* and *hint* are among them.

A sure way to keep the two straight is this: A person's statement never infers; it always implies. Inferring always goes on inside one's mind.

In order to

"Unnecessary!" reads the teacher comment accompanying the line drawn through the first two of these three words. That is always true when the phrase starts a sentence:

> ~~In order~~ to be heard, he stood on a bullhorn and shouted through a stepladder, but somehow it didn't seem to work.

But at other times deleting the words causes ambiguity:

> He pretended to be reluctant ~~in order~~ to show the problem that can cause a manager.

158

Lay, Lie et al

Despite the efforts of teachers, and the invention of all kinds of memory gimmicks, the confusion among *lay, lie, laying, lying* and so on will probably last as long as people write English. These are both incorrect:

> I left it laying on the table.
> I suppose somebody lay it there and forgot it.

After the first grade, people have little problem with the present tense: We lie down, we lay something else down. *Lie* transmits no action; *lay* always does. (*Now I lay me down to sleep* is, too, correct; it means *Now I lay myself down to sleep*.)

The problem between *to lie* and *to lay* seems to--er, lie in the fact that the word *lay* pops up both infinitive families. It is both the present tense of *to lay* and the past tense of *to lie*.

To summarize:

All forms of the infinitive *to lay* have the *A* sound. They all transmit action:

> I lay bricks today, I laid them yesterday, I have laid them, she lays them, we are laying them.

The *to lie* infinitive has mostly the *I* sound, with two exceptions (underlined). None of these words can transmit action:

> They lie down, he <u>lay</u> down yesterday, we have <u>lain</u> down for two hours, Bob lies down, we are none of us lying around.

To avoid the misuse of *lay*, the only word on both lists, use this correct model: *The bricks you will lay today lay on the floor yesterday.*

Number vs. Volume

Think of a bucket of water and a bucket of bolts. Their contents are clearly different--and you must measure them in different terms. Spill some of each. Is there now fewer water than there was before? Has the number of water decreased? Of course not.

Fewer and *number* are used for things--plurals. A thing, singular, must be described by *less* and *amount*. The misuse is probably careless, but it is common.

> We can't be expected to produce the same amount of sales with less salespeople. (*Make it* the same <u>number</u> of sales, <u>fewer</u> salespeople.)

159

Did you say something (possibly "Pardon me?")

Did you say something (possibly "Pardon me"?)

Did you say something (possibly "Pardon me?)"

Did you say something (possibly "Pardon me)"?

Did you say something (possibly "Pardon me)?"^*$^%$!#*

CLUSTERS OF PUNCTUATION at the end of a sentence can drive you crazy, if you let them.

(*But this is fine*) We can't be expected to produce the same amount of sales volume with less staff.

How about *quantity?* You're safe with that. It means either number or volume.

Punctuation Combination

Are any of these ending punctuations correct? Does it matter? The answers are: Yes, one is correct; no, it doesn't matter much-- excepting to those people who learned to do it right in school; and they are not going to let you ever forget it either, Buster.

> Did you say something (possibly "Pardon me?")
> Did you say something (possibly "Pardon me"?)
> Did you say something (possibly "Pardon me?)"
> Did you say something (possibly "Pardon me")?
> Did you say something (possibly "Pardon me)"?
> Did you say something (possibly "Pardon me)?"?!%#*!

The correct version is the fourth one.

Here are the guidelines for punctuation within parentheses and within quotations:

➥ Inside closing quotation marks:

Commas and periods go inside--always. Colons and semicolons go outside--always. These are arbitrary rules, but you violate them at your own peril. As to other punctuation--question marks, exclamation points and dashes--it is placed according to the context.

If those marks belong to the material quoted, they stay with it, and go inside the quotes. If they are not part of the quoted passage, they go outside the quotes. These are both correct:

> I enjoyed the movie "Tora! Tora! Tora!"
> Have you read the play "Love Letters"?

➥ With parentheses:

If the parenthesized material merely concludes a clause or sentence, the punctuation mark goes outside. If the entire sentence is in parentheses, the punctuation goes inside along with the words.

> He was right. (He always is, of course.)
> He was right (as he always is).
> If you want to (and I suppose you do), you may apply.

NOTE: A question mark never needs further punctuation, even in a spot where a comma would otherwise be correct.

> (*Correct*) When he said he would go, we all cheered.
> (*Correct*) When he said "Shall I go?" we all cheered.
> (*Incorrect*) When he said "Shall I go?," we all cheered.

What happens when quotation mark and parenthesis collide? The one containing the other must go on the outside. These are both correct:

> He said, "Please order two of the PY2 canisters (the blue ones)."
> (I hope he doesn't forget the PY2 "blue canisters.")

Shall

The world has almost passed *shall* by. It is left with only one useful function, to start a question:

> Shall we have each candidate come in separately?

But government agencies, especially, persist in using *shall* in ordinances when they mean *must* but don't want to sound too hamhanded. What too often happens is that readers wishfully read *shall* as discretionary (or pretend to), and pay no attention whatsoever to what is being ordained.

2B or Not Two Bee: Words or Numbers?

Numbers (and symbols also) are partially exempt from the laws of language. Grammar, schmammar; we need some other set of guidelines here. Numbers are not words.

But when they are considered as words, they may be treated grammatically. Most of them are adjectives: *three chairs, 1,234,333 visitors.* Some are nouns*: He counted to 100.* Some are pronouns: *The two sang a duet.* You can handle them in a sentence as you would any other word.

When you use numbers, you have only two related areas of concern:

✎ When do you spell them out; when do you use them as numerals?

✎ How do you make them easiest for the reader to absorb?

(We won't deal here with "accounting" use of numbers; I mean balance sheets, tabulations and so on that are almost entirely numerical. The standards they must meet are arithmetic, not linguistic.)

The first of your concerns--words vs. numerals--will be governed partly by long-set convention, partly by company preference, and partly by your own good judgment. The second--how to make them most readable--depends entirely on your judgment. But there are some guidelines you can use.

It's been found that generally numbers are most easily grasped when written as numbers--especially as they get longer. So an overall guideline is to use figures unless there is good reason not to. Then all we need to do is to think out what those good reasons might be.

➥ One, of course, is any arbitrary preference your organization may have. If the boss insists on *six percent* or *six %*, there is probably little point in your arguing that *6* works better, or that *per cent* is a more correct derivative of the Latin *per centum.*

It should go without saying that the company style should be consistent and logical.

163

•• Also, numbers written as figures tend to slow the reader's progression through a sentence--just as initials, acronyms, symbols, and other non-words do:

> The 13,445 fans watched as 8 hotrod speedsters raced 100 times around the 2-mile track at the August 7 MNC speedway opening. Winner "Boomboom" Carrera, 34, had won only 3 races before his victory here.

So three factors ought to guide your decision: When to spell out numbers and when to leave them alone? One is company preference; two, the fact that numbers are easier to understand as figures than as words; three--balancing that--the little visual roadbumps they provide the fast-reading reader.

Start with this principle: Use figures for those things that are inherently numerical. That means ages, weights and heights (in fact, most measurements), dollars, time, sizes, percentages, and the like.

That principle will often need to be balanced against principles of legibility and readability:

∞ Spell out numbers *one* through *nine*. When you get into multiple digits, switch to numbers. Thus: *one, two, three...**nine, 10**, 11....*

Use the same guideline for *first, second..**ninth, 10th,** 11th....*

Addresses also follow this rule. An address comprises a number and a street name, That name may be Sixth Street or Eighth Avenue. But it still is a name more than a number. So write:

> 123 Third Avenue
> Apt. 43-B, 11th Avenue

∞ Don't start a sentence with a numeral. Spell it out. Or, if the number is too large for that, use a Workaround and avoid the need to make the choice. Figures make very unconvincing sentence-starters, and sometimes look like decimals continuing the preceding sentence:

> ....and the market edged slightly upward. 153 stocks in our portfolio advanced....
> (*Better*) Of the stocks in our portfolio, 153 advanced....

∞ Don't mix numerals and words in sentences or lists.

Within a list, put them all in figures. That's also best within a sentence also, but sometimes it gets difficult.

If you have begun your sentence with a spelled-out word, it's okay to have all other numbers in the list written numerically. But that means all of them. Don't write:

> Three players scored more than once: Smith, 12 times; Crawshaw, 11 times, and Wilson, three times.

In this case, since the numbers are very close, they would read well as either words or figures. If they are a related pair, mixing is okay *(he hit eight of 12 free throws).* If the numbers differ widely--4, 568, 45, 2--it's better to use figures. As a rule, once you have to start hyphenating the word (*twenty-one*), you're better off using figures.

☞ If you have a choice, and you usually do, avoid roman numerals. They are harder to read than arabic ones. You can find section CVII all right, but it will take a little thought.

☞ These are pretty standard places to use figures:

Rulings and votes (*the Court voted 5 to 4*); odds and ratios (*6 to 1 odds, 20:1 ratio*); most sequential word-and-number combinations (*Act 2, Channel 5, 8 on the Richter scale, English 6),* and sports scores (*the Reds won 4-3*--but write *seventh hole, three-pointer, hit three for four*).

☞ And here are some traditional places to use words instead:

In indefinite usage (*a hundred per cent wrong, in his seventies, increased twentyfold*); figures of speech (*a thousand and one ways, Ten Commandments, I've told you a million times)*; fractions below one if they stand alone (*half an inch*) but not if they are joined to something else (*a 1/2-inch pipe),* and unrelated figures bumping into each other (*ten 15-room units*).

➜ To decrease the line resistance in your sentence--to help the reader read--you may find some of these approaches useful:

- ➜ Round off large numbers if they are as meaningful as the precise ones would be--and use a figure-word combination:

> The company's $4.8 million Workers Compensation payment. (*So what if it really is $4,790,009.38?*)

- ➜ Avoid shoving numbers together if you can separate them:

> (*Hard to read*) Of the 18, 17 voted to abstain.
> (*Easier*) Seventeen of the 18 voted to abstain.

- ➜ Don't use *approximately* with exact figures.

Any errors you make in number style are unlikely to harm your meaning. On the other hand, having a surefooted approach to them is good for your self-image, and helps impart a shipshape look to your writing that readers will like.

The main things to remember about number style:

1. It should match that of your organization--if it has an established preference.

2. Above all, it should be consistent--certainly within a given document, ideally across all documents. When you come across an oddball case and you must decide on the style, make a note of how you handled it. Otherwise, when it occurs again you may have forgotten.

3. And, when in doubt, trust common sense. I close with an example whose writer must have forgotten to do this. You'll have to take my word that this example is verbatim:

> Of the 2,222 northbound hauls, approximately one-half (or 1,111) resulted in empty return trips.

Think. Always think.

CHAPTER 16

Speling

There is a surefire way to cure poor spelling. A friend of mine guarantees it. You take a couple of cotton wads soaked with carbon tet, place them inside the burrow, toss in a match and....No, that's for moles.

Poor spelling is like moles, though, in that everyone seems to have his or her own foolproof cure. They range from contrived and hard-to-remember memory devices to changing your major to linguistics.

Some things work, some don't. I knew a welder who misspelled a quarter of the few words he wrote. But he never misspelled the toughie *acetylene.* He was, as you'd guess, an acetylene welder. The point is, if spelling matters enough, most people will spell reasonably well. But English is probably the hardest language to spell; for many people it's more trouble than it is worth.

How much does it matter? Here is one textbook's grim view:

> Correct spelling is absolutely essential in business communications.
> It is taken for granted and expected at all times; therefore, no
> one should be satisfied with anything less than perfection.

Come off it. Absolutely essential? Taken for granted at all times? Walk up to a businessperson with a letter in your hand. Ask him or her to lay a wager, either way, on whether the letter contains a spelling error. If the person bets on perfection, I owe you lunch.

The truth is, few messages are free of misspellings. Some have more than others. And--it's true--those glitches do cause some readers to think less of you. And anyone can catch spelling errors, even poor spellers. (My welder friend would notice if you misspelled *acetylene.*) So you ought not make too many.

The same book alleges, "Spelling errors also cost your company money," but it doesn't say how. Oh, they could, I suppose, if you spelled *voltmeter* a-n-v-i-l and ordered 1000 of them. But as a money drain it ranks somewhere below extended coffee breaks.

Spelling is a funny thing. (Misspelling, of course, is not.) It seems not to relate more than generally to intelligence or to other verbal ability. It does correlate with memory, and with pattern-recognition skills. Some people are probably natural spellers.

CLIENTELE
Is hard to spele
And, furthermore,
it sounds like hele.
Clients will work
just as wele.

(And sound less affected
to boot.)

ONE USAGE BOOK lists "1064 Commonly Misspelled Words." Among them is "iguana."
Taking their word for it--think of the billions of dollars this error must cost US industry.

But there is also hope for the rest. Spelling can greatly improve if you work at it. You really need to know that. Otherwise your efforts will be half-hearted and probably unsuccessful.

The best ways to get better are mechanical and not very profound. One of the very best is, when you catch a misspelling, to write it correctly 100 times. Chances are good that the next time-- back on the job--it will also be correct.

To test that system, have someone read you the word a week later and see whether you spell it right. Probably you will; if not, repeat the 100-word drill.

How do you catch those errors? If you use a software spellcheck program it will flag most misspellings, and even suggest the correct way. That's good news and bad. The good news is that your memo is freer of misspellings. The bad news is that you may just insert the correct spelling without "grooving it"; that is, imbedding it in your mind so you'll spell it right next time.

Lacking a software program, you might seek other help. Find a good speller, and "hire" that person to review your written material for some period of time, marking all spelling errors. Or, he or she can supplement your software spellchecker by catching common errors an electronic eye would miss, such as sound-alike words (*their* for *they're*, *do to* for *due to*.)

(Spellcheckers also miss errors in punctuation, odd spacing, omitted words--and misused words. You could mistype *The small man had a big ego* as *The swell men hid a bug egg* and the computer would okay it, since the words are all good.)☛

Then take a further step: Categorize those errors. Do you misspell many words, or just a few? Are most misspellings sound-alike words? Do you misspell consistently--or do you spell a word one way one time, another way another time? Are your misspellings mostly new words, or those you've known for years?

This kind of categorizing doesn't take much time, and can yield useful results. For instance, most people are surprised how few words they really misspell; they typically exaggerate their spelling problem. So right away you've cut it down to size; it seems more manageable. And is.

☛Another--surprisingly common--problem is the sloppiness of some spellcheck software. I use two programs. One of them failed to recognize *leniency* and suggested substituting *lennie*. Another flashed the error signal on *can't's* and suggested *pant's*; it also wanted to change *dying* (correct) to *dieing* (wrong). So you need now and then to show it who's boss.

In general, use of memory joggers to remember correct spelling works best if you make up your own. Otherwise it's like trying to wear someone else's clothes. Here's a (serious) suggestion from *Simon and Schuster's Handbook for Writers*--a way to remember how to spell immigrant and emigrant:

"An emigrant l**e**aves and an immigrant comes **in**."

The idea, if you can believe it, is to tie the **e** in **e**migrant to the **e** in l**e**aves and the **i** in immigrant to the **i** in **in**.

My hunch is that most mnemonics are too complicated. If a person can't remember how to spell pig, he or she is unlikely to recall the memory phrase Porkers Ingest Grain.

Classifying your errors helps you focus your attack. Suppose you find that you misspell sound-alike words, let's say *pain* for *pane or threw* for *through*. Then when you write it correctly 100 times, be sure to include a tie-in (*window pane* or *follow through*) to link the word to its correct usage.

Or you may find your misspelling sounds right to you. That may suggest an error in pronunciation (*differnt* for *different*, for instance). Then, as you learn to say it right, it will reinforce your correct spelling.

Most important: Keep track of your progress. Tally your errors monthly, and the incidence of specific misspelled words. You'll soon notice that the total number is dropping, and that you're spelling certain words correctly each time. That's a very good feeling.

Don't be impatient if progress is slow or erratic. It took you decades to develop your misspellings; it may take weeks to unlearn them.

Also, many misspellings are due to carelessness, writing in haste and not rereading carefully. Another part of the problem is wordiness. As you write more simply, you'll use easier-to-spell words, and avoid embarrassing sentences such as this:

The situation is contributed to (*attributed to*) parental neglect.

Writing instead *The situation is due to parental neglect* would have solved that person's "spelling problem."

Re-read with a critical eye. Write in simple language. Get electronic or human help in flagging your errors. Classify those misspellings, and focus your attack accordingly. Rewrite the correct versions over and over until they're "grooved." Settle, if need be, for modest but continuous improvement.

Your spelling will get better.

CHAPTER 17

Capital Offenses

The worst problem with capitalizing is not doing it wrong. The worst problem is doing it too much.

Some writers seem to believe that capital letters make what's being said more important. They don't. The real value of capitals--like that of any usage element--is to make something more readily understandable.

The good news is that capitalization falls mostly into two categories:

➧ Standard usage that you've learned by now: Capitalize the start of a sentence. Capitalize proper names, of anything from people to countries. And so on; I'll run a short summary later.

➧ Specific preferences of your company, your editor or your boss. (You'll be unlikely to find any formal listing of such preferences, but you can nose around or dig them out through conversations.) Add them to the style guidebook you're compiling. You are compiling one, are you not (Chapter 4)? If not, a mild tsk! for you.

This is the most important thing to know about capitalizing: More than any other aspect of writing, it is subjective--prey to the whim of individual companies, editors and bosses. They will think of their choices not as arbitrary but as matters of right or wrong, but that is seldom the case.

That leaves you with only two problem areas:

➧ Oddball things that don't fit general guidelines. I'll cover some of them in this chapter.

➧ The tendency to overcapitalize. That is the worst problem. "Overcapping" is, and often appears, amateurish--a flailing to achieve emphasis. It doesn't work.

Here are three sound guidelines for capitalizing:

1. When in doubt, don't.
2. Ask, would the sentence mean anything different if the words were lowercased (not capitalized)? If it would, or even might, keep the capital letters.
3. Once you make a choice, stick with it in all instances.

171

Taking the three individually:

1. When in doubt, don't capitalize. This is the preference of most magazines and newspapers--and most professional writers. That is why, over the years, capitalization has decreased--in that realm.

It is **not** the preference of most companies and agencies--who have, if anything, increased the amount of capitalization they use. For no good reason, I might add. So, if you are a determined lower-caser, you may have a fight on your hands.

Lawyers and their groupies have contributed to capital overuse:

> Father Knows Wurst Sausage Company (hereinafter referred to as The Company) maintains that Wilferd D. Frudd (hereinafter referred to as The Plaintiff)...

It could as easily say:

> Father Knows Wurst Sausage Company (hereinafter, the company) maintains that Wilferd D. Frudd (hereinafter, the plaintiff)...

Does such capitalized defining simplify either the writing or the reader's understanding? I doubt it. Newspapers, for instance, manage to describe equally complex proceedings without leaning on artificial capitals:

> The company maintained that the plaintiff was....

Using the capitalized name can spawn further awkward writing, as in this corporate annual report:

> The Company believes that no competitor in any of The Company's market areas offers a wider variety of products than The Company.

Far easier to read:

> The company believes that in its market areas no competitor offers a wider variety of products.

Organizations fall into the trap of inflating everything from job titles to departments to you name it:

> Glenda Freep, District Manager at our Minot, N.D. Field Office, has been promoted to Assistant Sales Director in the Miscellaneous Stuff Division. She will be responsible for Retail and Discounted Sales.

The following version would lose nothing but a few big letters:

172

> Glenda Freep, district manager at our Minot, N.D. field office, has
> been promoted to assistant sales director in the Miscellaneous
> Stuff division. She will be responsible for retail and discounted sales.

With the wider typeface choices now offered by computer software, we may be in for even more-mindless word inflation:

> Glenda Freep, District Manager, has been promoted to
> **A**ssistant **S**ales **D**irector...

Government agencies just love capitals:

> Upon filling out the Application Form, the Applicant must furnish the
> Recruitment Office with proof of previous employment. The Recruiting
> Officer will then...

These organizations also are given to using exclamation points, senseless underlining and use of all-capitals.

> Fill out BOTH FORMS and place <u>each one</u> in its designated slot.
> IMPORTANT: <u>Do not</u> separate the carbon from the ORIGINAL!

This doomsday tone would unnerve the typical applicant to the point that he or she would probably slop ink and mess up everything.

There are already enough uses for capitals. You don't need to invent more.

2. Ask, would the sentence mean anything different if the words were lower-cased ? If it would, or even might, keep the capital letters. Otherwise, drop them.

> I spoke to the president on the phone
> I spoke to the President on the phone.

In the second example you would keep the capital. The capitalized version, by custom, means the President of the United States. (That custom is changing, however.)

> (*No*) The new Field Office will be constructed in Puzzley, N.J.
> (*Yes*) He has a new position in Marketing.

The first sentence makes the same sense with or without the big F and O; drop them. The second, however, should keep the capitals, since marketing as a professional field and Marketing as a company department are different.

3. Once you make a choice, stick with it.

Don't shilly-shally or excuse exceptions. If you describe your own job as *Director* of Lobbying, don't describe someone else's as *director* of Public Relations or *manager* of Governmental Affairs. They have the capital coming if you do. Better yet is not to use it for anyone.

One of the harder areas is capitalization of job titles. There are two sub-problems: Capitalizing or not before a proper name (*President John Smith*) and capitalizing or not after a proper name or in its absence (*a talk by the president of the college*). Some of this will be mandated by your organization. If not, you must fend for yourself.

1. Titles before the name: You would write *President Mary Keller of Sew What? Needle Company.* You would not write *Janitor's Assistant Bunky Schweff of Sew What? Needle Company.* So at what point do you stop? Some books say to capitalize "titles but not job descriptions." But the dividing line is fuzzy. Is D(d)irector of Personnel a title? How about S(s)upervisor of Word Processing? How about V(v)ice-president of Finance? How about A(a)ssistant V(v)ice- president of Finance?

Here is one often-useful guideline: Would you naturally refer to, or introduce, the person by title and last name? If so, a capital is appropriate: *President Keller, Sheriff Diddley, Sergeant Hruba.* If not, the capital is silly: *Dogcatcher Ketchum, Auditor Beedy, Messenger Boy Slade.*

Common sense ought also enter into your choice. Avoid awkwardness:

> I enjoyed the remarks of Assistant Vice-President of International
> Corporate Affairs Burley Furley.

There it is wisest to put the title after the name. As a matter of fact, there are really few times when you must precede the name with the title anyway.

2. Titles after the name. By custom, titles following names (or in the absence of names) are not capitalized, unless they are unique, like these:

> The President of the United States, the Pope, the Great One (Jackie
> Gleason), the Sultan of Swat (Babe Ruth)

How about using all-capitals to emphasize a word? Capitalizing is one of the clumsier ways to provide emphasis. The best way is to do so by the way you use the word:

> He hit the sidewalk--hard.

Most were slow and lumbering, but not Smith. He was fast.
Eager is the word for Bennie Drooble.

Or by typographical variation:

He hit the sidewalk <u>hard</u>
He hit the sidewalk **hard.**
He hit the sidewalk *hard*.

Go easy on all-caps used in narrative text. THEY'RE HARD TO READ, ESPECIALLY IN QUANTITY. (AREN'T THEY?) THEY LOOK BLOCKY. THEY'RE HARD TO PROOFREAD. AND THEY SOMETIMES BECOME CONFUSED WITH INITIAL GROUPS AND ACRONYMS:

Please HOLD all NASA photos until Saturday.
DO use DNA records. DO NOT use DOA records.

Much easier reading:

<u>Please hold</u> all NASA photos until Saturday.
Use DNA records. Do <u>not</u> use DOA records.

☞ Here, in a nutshell, are the standard uses of capitals:

☞ Capitalize words that are referred to as names: person, place, product, company, deity, day of the week, etc. You know most of them:

✻ Betty Jones, Strom Berry, Walter Mellon, Minnie Syllable, Ed Koch, Mother (*but lowercase* his mother)...
✻ Goose Valley, New York, the Washington Monument, Empire State Building, the Midwest (*but* a midwest state), Sunset Boulevard, Spanish...
✻ Pepsi-Cola, Ole-Olayhee! Swiss-Mexican food, Puppy Snacks...
✻ God (*but lowercase* a Greek god)
✻ Andersen Company (*but lowercase* the company)
✻ Constitution, Taft-Hartley Act...
✻ Friday, January (*but lowercase* fall, winter)
✻ U.S. Government (*but lowercase* government, state, city, federal)

☞ Capitalize *The* only if it is part of an official name:

The Hague, The Shadows, The McLaughlin Group....*but* the Pyramids, the Middle East, the Marketing department, the World Series

(Should *department* above be capitalized? Some authorities say no; it is the generic part of the proper name, like *Columbia river, Northern hemisphere*. But it's a matter of company preference, and

176

most companies like capitals. I prefer it down--that is, lowercased: *the Marketing department;* but I'm in the shriveling minority on this one.)

And, for humor or special emphasis, you may wish to capitalize:

> Dating Gloria deSmedley was considered to be A Big Deal.
> He was a foe of Big Government.

∞ When you quote someone--which doesn't occur a lot in your writing--capitalize the first word of each sentence quoted. But if you're quoting only part of a sentence, or continuing a sentence, don't capitalize the first word. The following are all correct:

> "I am fed up with this hay," the horse said.
> "I'll be darned!" said the cow. "It's a talking horse!" (*Quoting two
> separate sentences.*)
> "The reason I am fed up," the horse said, "is that I ate brunch too late."
> (*One sentence continued in separate portions.*)
> The horse said he was "fed up" with the hay. (*Sentence only partly
> quoted.*)

∞ Lowercase plurals even if the word would be capitalized when singular:

> Multnomah and Clackamas counties (*but* Multnomah County), First
> to Eighth streets (*but* First Street), Fifth and Seventh amendments

∞ Capitalize the first letter of each sentence.

∞ Capitalize the first letter of each sentence that follows a colon. Lowercase any non-sentence following a colon, however long that portion gets. All these are right:

> He had a good idea: Allow welfare recipients to cut trash trees in
> areas to be clearcut.
> There is only one rule: Play fair. (*Sentence follows colon.*)
> We could offer an incentive: free Cracker-Jacks to every engineer
> who keeps his workbench tidy. (*Non-sentence follows colon.*)

But lowercase the first word of a parenthesized sentence within another sentence.

> The pace of change in microchip development (you ain't seen nothin'
> yet!) puts great demands on R&D labs.

➡Lowercase words that were once proper names but have taken on secondary and unrelated meanings:

manhattan (cocktail), french toast, gothic (meaning gloomy), biblical, brussels sprouts, oriental rug, swiss cheese **but**--*wave flag here*-**American** cheese!

And if all the above advice fails, remember the very best of all:

When in doubt as to whether to capitalize, don't. Just say No.

Or, perhaps, no.

CHAPTER 18

Cadence and Logic: Punctuation

Concise writing needs little punctuation. Wordy writing usually requires a lot. What's more, short sentences are easy to punctuate, longer ones harder. The careless writer who commits a 50-word sentence may get the vague feeling that there ought to be a few pauses in there somewhere. So, with a prayer, he plops in a comma or two.

After-the-fact punctuation seldom works very well. The comma is as likely to stop the reader who's going strong as it is to assist the one who is bogging down. One long idea is better than two half-ideas.

You need to insert punctuation while you write, not as an editorial afterthought. What you have learned in this book about phrases and clauses will help a lot; it will let you place punctuation pauses where they will help your reader most.

Fortunately (if you are writing on your own) or unfortunately (if you are under the thumb of a dictatorial editor), very little agreement exists on where those pause marks should go. The rules of punctuation are:

Rule 1: A period goes at the end of a sentence that makes a statement.

Rule 2: A question mark goes at the end of a genuine question. (But not an indirect question; for instance, this is incorrect: "He asked where the bathroom was?")☛

Rule 3: There are hardly any other rules.

What remain are preferences. Some of them are arbitrary and by now pretty standard; you know them without a tedious review: Commas used in dates, after salutations and before quotations; quotation marks around quotations; periods for abbreviations, and so on.

Most problems arise in the sentence's midsection. There a misplaced punctuation mark can impair not only the cadence of the words but also the structure of the logic. Most of those misplaced marks are commas.

> "It may almost be said that what reads wrongly if the punctuation is removed is radically bad."
>
> --H. W. Fowler

☛ (Unless this was the situation:) "Where the bathroom was?" Lyczsinksi asked.

Writers tend to use less and less punctuation all the time. Since each mark would slow or stop the reader, this trend should make for faster reading. That is, provided that the message is clear without that kind of help. Too often it is not.

But reducing punctuation can't be done by just cutting the number of marks in half. Those that do nothing but prop up feeble prose should be cut out. (Better yet, cut out the feeble prose.) But, when punctuation is used to clarify a message, retaining it does your reader a favor.

Sentences pockmarked with punctuation are usually sentences so muddled as to require rewriting.

PERIODS

Periods are the worst problem: Writers use too few of them. Cut your average sentence length 25 per cent and I predict you will reduce your punctuation errors 50 per cent.

Other than that, you probably handle periods just fine. The only occasional question I am asked is: When I end a sentence with an abbreviation, do I use one period or two? Is this right or wrong?

I was introduced to Marcus Welby, M.D..

Use just one period. Using two makes it look like your word processor stuttered, and readers will mentally edit the second one.

COMMAS

A comma is an extra breath between two words. Some comma rules have been mandatory for so long that you know them by heart. Others are discretionary; you are free to put a comma in whenever you think a pause will keep your reader on track.

Commas are the biggest punctuation headache, accounting for more problems than all the other marks combined. There are two reasons: (1) You use more of them; (2) Their misuse may cause the most serious problems.

Commas have two basic jobs. They are different enough that they deserve two different marks. But we only have one. The uses are:

∞ Showing that something is omitted. Usually it is the word *and*. Second most common is the word *that*. Sometimes the omission is a word or group of words that are understood in spite of their absence; for example:

> The Council ruled that policemen would receive a 3 per cent
> raise; firemen, 5 per cent. (*Comma stands for* would receive).

✍ Setting off material from the clause. This set-off material will be a **commenting** word, clause or phrase (Chapter 10). This sentence contains one of each:

> In a press conference,/ President Bush once discussed his least-favorite
> vegetable,/ broccoli,/ which a reporter had asked about.
> (*commenting phrase, commenting word, commenting clause.*)

On the other hand, <u>defining</u> words, phrases and clauses should never be set off with commas. This sentence contains one of each:

> The man /who wrote the novel /"Wuthering"/ never rose to the
> heights/ expected of him. (*defining clause, defining word,*
> *defining phrase.*)

Taking the two uses in order:

☞ **Showing that something is left out.** In a series or list, the comma between items substitutes for *and.*

> I would like four packages of printer paper, four XC11
>   ribbons, three....
> I would like four packages of printer paper **and** four XC11
>   ribbons **and** three....

There are two exceptions to this use. One is arbitrary, the other is logical:

1. A comma before the final *and* in a comma-separated series:

> The flag was red, white, and blue.

The final comma is a small redundancy, making the translated series read:

> The flag was red and white <u>and and</u> blue. (*One "and"* already was there;
> *the comma provides the second.*)

For most of my life I have been a dedicated no-comma-before-*and* advocate. But style preferences are changing, and the trend is clearly toward including the comma. The purpose is to avoid confusion when the next-to-last item in a series is itself a compound, as here:

> "You put in stops to help your reader understand you, not to please grammarians. And you should write so that person will understand you with a minimum of help of that sort."
>
>   --Sir Ernest Gowers

> Photos included those of Dwight Eisenhower, Albert Einstein,
> Abbott and Costello, and Queen Elizabeth.

2. Commas between cumulative items in a list of modifiers. Both the next lists are okay, despite the difference in comma treatment:

> She bought a shiny new red LeBaron convertible.
> He made an awkward, unexpected, forceful movement with the pole.

What is the difference? The first series is cumulative. Each modifier builds on, reinforces, the one following it. It was a convertible. It was a LeBaron convertible. It was a red LeBaron convertible. It was a new red LeBaron convertible. It was, in fact, a shiny new red LeBaron convertible.

By contrast, the second series lists distinct characteristics that do not reinforce one another.

One common, if imperfect, test is: Would the word *and* naturally fit between the items? If so, use a comma. If not, don't.

Also, for some reason, the sequence of the items seems to have some bearing on the need or lack of need for the comma. Otherwise why would we write:

> "Ringading" was a clever new musical. *(No comma.)*
> *(but)*
> "Ringading" was a new, clever musical. *(Comma seems needed.)*

So it comes down to a matter of ear. Trust yours. And any boss who says his is better is not an old, cranky tyrant. He is a cranky old tyrant.

☞ **Setting off material from the clause.** In determining whether something should or should not be separated from the rest of the sentence, it sometimes helps to ask: Would this word/phrase/clause look appropriate either inside parentheses or set off by dashes? If it would, it is a commenting rather than a defining element and should be set off by commas.

The most common problem is an interruptive element. It needs two commas; often only one is inserted. That is like putting in only one parenthesis--a (without a). Here are some incorrect examples:

> Let me know whether an adjustment is being made or if not,
> why it is not.
> Must Gilroy as a co-owner of the surface-mode patents, be joined
> in the Johnson v. Techco lawsuit?

182

DeVito attempts the fight of his life against Ms. Sullivan and
   most important, Ms. Sullivan's daughter.
It is the best, if not the only book on slug farming.

A common place to omit the set-off comma is after a conjunction
that already has a comma in front of it:

The last quarter did show increased earnings, but in spite of
the growth, we are only cautiously optimistic about the
immediate future. (*Comma needed after* but, *to set off the phrase*
in spite of.)

How to guard against this common problem? Here's a useful
guideline: **Cross out the set-off material bounded by commas--or by
a comma and one end of the sentence.   The message that remains
should express a complete idea and have no leftover portions**. Each
of the above examples would fail that test:

Let me know whether an adjustment is being made or if not,
   ~~why it is not~~.
~~Must Gilroy as a co-owner of the surface-mode patents~~, be joined
   in the Johnson v. Techco lawsuit?
DeVito attempts the fight of his life against Ms. Sullivan and
   most important, ~~Ms. Sullivan's daughter.~~
~~It is the best~~, if not the only book on slug farming.
The last quarter did show increased earnings, ~~but in spite of
   the grow~~th, we are only cautiously optimistic about the
   immediate future. (*This one comes close, but loses the
   critical connector* but.)

Each of these revised examples would have passed the test:

Let me know whether an adjustment is being made or, ~~if not,~~
   why it is not.
Must Gilroy, ~~as a co-owner of the surface-mode patents~~, be joined
   in the Johnson v. Techco lawsuit?
DeVito attempts the fight of his life against Ms. Sullivan and,
   ~~most important~~, Ms. Sullivan's daughter.
It is the best, ~~if not the only~~, book on slug farming.
The last quarter did show increased earnings, but, ~~in spite of
   the growth,~~ we are only cautiously optimistic about the
   immediate future.

✏ If a sentence contains two main clauses that go in different direc-
tions, you need a comma before the conjunction. These connectors
signal such sentences: *but, not, nor.* If the two clauses do not aim
different ways, the comma is discretionary. Unless the sentence is
short, I prefer to use the comma. All the following examples are
okay:

*"Dear Mr. Language
Person: What is the
purpose of the
apostrophe?"*

"A. The apostrophe is
used mainly in hand-
lettered business signs to
alert the reader that an 'S'
is coming up at the end
of a word, as in:
WE DO NOT ACCEPT
PERSONAL CHECK'S, or:
NOT RESPONSIBLE FOR
ANY ITEM'S."
                --Dave Barry

183

The team is now five years old, but this is the first year it has
paid its players.

He was not clever, nor was he particularly brave.

It was very windy and the building shook. (*Comma after* windy *is
also okay.*)

If no word joins the two clauses, you have two sentences and
need at least a semicolon to connect them. Trying to make a comma do that job causes the notorious "comma splice"; for instance:

(*Incorrect*) He told her he was a professional automobile driver, he was
really a cabbie from the Bronx.

(*All acceptable:*)

He told her he was a professional automobile driver; he was
really a cabbie from the Bronx.

He told her he was a professional automobile driver. He was
really a cabbie from the Bronx.

He told her he was a professional automobile driver, but he was
really a cabbie from the Bronx.

✏ A long phrase that precedes a main clause should be followed by
a comma. Even better: Don't put long phrases in that position. A
reader shouldn't have to read more than six or eight words to know
the subject of the sentence.

Usually the same phrase placed at the end of the sentence would
not need a comma before it.

Because of management support in the early stages of the basic research
program, the project moved along with adequate financing.

(*Also correct:*)

The project moved along with adequate financing because of
management support in the early stages of the basic research program.

✏ A prepositional, gerund, participial or infinitive phrase (chapter
10) preceding the main clause needs to be followed by a comma:

For instance, you might find yourself in need of ready cash.

Leaping into the stands, he made a bare-handed catch.

✏ The comma has enough to do; don't give it additional jobs, such
as pretending to be a colon.

The comma is versatile. One big job is separating items in a
series. Another is setting off an *appositive,* a word or group of words
that renames a noun. Using an appositive is like saying *in other
words* or *who is.*

He introduced his mother, one of the world's top tuba players.

But make sure your reader knows which of the two above ways your comma is being used. Here there is some doubt:

He introduced his three brothers, two jugglers, and a knife thrower.

How many people were introduced? It might be six. It is only three, however, as the colon in this corrected example shows:

He introduced his three brothers: two jugglers and a knife thrower.

THE SEMICOLON

A semicolon looks like what it is, half comma and half period. And that's just how it is used, to make the reader pause a bit longer than a comma would, but not as long as a period would.

The good news is: If semicolons give you fits, you can go through life writing well without ever using one.

There is one exception: It is a Supercomma, very handy when you want to separate a series whose items themselves contain commas:

The job involves public contact, press relations and financial relations, governmental affairs, political relations and lobbying, and external media contact.
(*Clearer*) The job involves public contact, press relations and financial relations; governmental affairs; political relations and lobbying; and external media contact.

The job thus divides into four responsibilities instead of seven.

A cautionary note: A semicolon is not a colon. It does not introduce anything--ever.

THE COLON

The colon goes ta-<u>daa!</u> It is a trumpet fanfare introducing something. That something may be a list or a quotation; equally often it is the punctuational equivalent of *that is*:

Two things are needed to become a millionaire overnight: brilliant investment skill and a bank account with $999,999 in it.

The colon (unless introducing a bulleted list) shouldn't interrupt a clause, as this one does:

To get ahead you need: drive and intelligence.

"The correct use of the comma--if there is such a thing as 'correct use'--can only be acquired by observation, common sense and taste."

--Sir Ernest Gowers

Capitalize a complete statement that follows a colon; lowercase any partial statement, including a list of any length.

> Sherman said it: War is hell.
> Please send the following 54 items: a bucket of bolts, three sadirons,
> a deck of cards, a tub of lard.....

Introduce all direct quotations except short ones with a colon. What is short? You make the call.

THE EXCLAMATION POINT

<u>Instruction 1 for using an exclamation point</u> (or whiz-bang, in proofreader terminology):

Type 10 lines of exclamation points: !!!!!!!!!!!!!!!!!!!!!!!!!!!!!!!!!!! and so on.

<u>Instruction 2</u>: Now that you have them out of your system, never use another one in on-the-job writing.

Any statement amazing enough to justify a whiz-bang is amazing enough to get along without one. Any other statement doesn't deserve one.

DASHES AND PARENTHESES

These marks are more alike than unlike. In a bind, you could use commas for either of them--but commas have too many uses already.

Both marks set off material not intended to be part of the main thought. Parentheses have one advantage: When you put down the (, you not only signal to the reader that a) is coming; you also remind yourself, and so are less likely to forget the). But, since a beginning dash (--) looks just like an ending dash (--), it's easy to think you've just ended an interruption when in truth you've just begun one.

This is a problem, of course, only when your sentence gets long and involved. But it can happen:

> The health network serves three states--Oregon, Idaho, and
> northern Washington--including Seattle.

Here the dash after *Washington* appears to be the partner of the one before *Oregon* But if you cross out the words enclosed by the dashes, you are left with a misleading sentence:

> The health network serves three states including Seattle.

Better to use a colon before the first interruption:

> The health network serves three states: Oregon, Idaho, and
> northern Washington--including Seattle.

When it is not used in pairs, the dash generally shows a breaking off of the thought or a summing up at the end of a sentence:

> There were insults, catcalls, boos--you get the idea.
> There is one small obstacle to his academic progress--his brain.

Parentheses neither break off an idea nor summarize. They inject comments or explanations that are clearly "asides" from the main thought. They should not be so far aside, however, that the reader can see no connection. That is, don't introduce an additional fact by wedging it into a sentence to which it is unrelated, as is done here:

> This moving drama (it was produced on a low budget and with
> an amateur cast) is set in the French countryside following World War II.

THE QUESTION MARK

A question appears after a direct question, but not after an indirect one:

> What is your preference?
> I wonder whether we misunderstood his instructions.

When the question is inside a quotation, the question mark goes inside the final quote marks. But if the quotation is inside the question, the ? goes outside the ".

> "How is everything?" sniveled the waiter, three seconds after
> setting our main course in front of us.
> Would you like one of our "Mike's Cafe specials"?

QUOTATION MARKS

There are few legitimate reasons to use quote marks. But writers are good at inventing illegitimate ones. The real uses are to write something word for word the way someone said it; to set off book titles, chapter names and so on when italics are not being used, and to mark a word or phrase used in some special way.

But it should be a really special way. If the word as you are using it would be clear to your reader without quotes, leave them off. That means leave them off most of the time. Otherwise you will appear to be using slang and apologizing for it at the same time.

"If you take hyphens seriously, you will surely go mad."

--Oxford University Press style book

187

Avoid this kind of thing:

> If you ask me, I think the fight had been "fixed."
> Ed, you "sly dog," you had us all fooled.
> The engineers needed two weeks to get the "bugs" out of the
> new circuit board.

I advise you to limit your quoting to whole sentences and full paragraphs, and hold down the use of partial quotes. This newspaper excerpt gets sort of silly.

> Burrard, known for his salty humor and robust language, was relaxed throughout the interview. He said the Gulf War was a "valuable experience" even though he wasn't sure the US should have "acted alone."

Wowee. What a fun evening it would be to listen to more of that salty robust feller. Limit your partial quotes to things said in a unique or interesting way, or statements for which you would prefer not to take responsibility.

THE APOSTROPHE

The apostrophe has three uses.

1. It pluralizes figures, letters, or words cited as words (*there are too many __whereas's__ in this contract*). But you would write, *No ifs, ands or buts,* since you are talking about an idea, not the literal words.

2. It replaces an omitted letter in a contraction (*it's, don't, rock 'n' roll*) or occasionally a commonly shortened word (*'way down South*).

(These two guidelines combined make it sound like you have to describe more than one *don't* as a two-apostrophe *don't's.* You do.)

Numbers 2 and 3 sometimes are confused.

3. It makes a noun or pronoun possessive. Normally you add an *'s* to the noun or pronoun: *cat's, everybody's.* That is usually the practice even with a proper noun--a name--even if it already ends in *s.* So you have *James's, Jones's, Thomas's.*

What is strongly frowned on is tagging an *'s* onto a word with two soft sounds already ending it. Avoid, for instance, *Texas's, princess's, molasses's.*

Plurals of nouns ending in *s* merely add the apostrophe to become possessive: *ladies' dresses, boys' basketball.*

A personal pronoun never takes an apostrophe. *Its, hers, theirs.*

Here is a tip that is worth the price of this entire book:

One of the great social dividing lines in our culture (undiscovered except by me) is the gap between those who can not get it straight whether to write *its* or *it's*, and those who would rather point out that error than eat steak. My survey is that our population is about equally divided along these lines.

The confusion is understandable. Why, the *its*-dummy reasons, if the possessive of *cat* is *cat's* and that of *company* is *company's*, should not the possessive of *it* be *it's?*

Grammatical answer: because it isn't. That's how grammar works.

Anyway, *it's* means *it is* or sometimes *it has* (as in *It's been great.*) As a memory jogger▰ for the millions of *its*-sufferers, I offer this:

If you were to inspect the word *it's* under a microscope, here is what you would see:

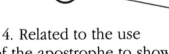

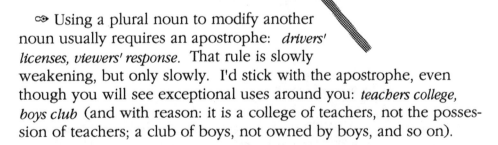

4. Related to the use of the apostrophe to show possession are two other uses:

☞ Using a plural noun to modify another noun usually requires an apostrophe: *drivers' licenses, viewers' response.* That rule is slowly weakening, but only slowly. I'd stick with the apostrophe, even though you will see exceptional uses around you: *teachers college, boys club* (and with reason: it is a college of teachers, not the possession of teachers; a club of boys, not owned by boys, and so on).

☞ Measuring time and space requires an apostrophe--most of the time: *two weeks' pay, 40 hours' practice, a hair's breadth.*

Most of the time doesn't mean all of the time. Some word pairs have become so united that the apostrophe is left out, such as *50 pounds pressure.* But most of the time is enough of the time. You can't get into trouble sticking with the apostrophe.

▰ I know I said they usually are worthless. But...heh heh...

THE HYPHEN

Hyphens differ from other punctuation marks in that they are not pause marks; they actually pull two words a bit closer together. They are by all agreement necessary evils; I'm not sure which of those words to stress.

What rules do exist allow many exceptions. You are pretty free to use them as your judgment dictates. One use is to avoid ambiguity.

A five-inch gun crew is made of midgets; *a five-inch-gun crew* is probably not. *We need more capable engineers* is not the same thing as *we need more-capable engineers;* nor *a small-women's store* the same *as a small women's store.*

In such modifier series, when one modifies another rather than the noun, show that connection with a hyphen. We do it automatically with some words already (*a pea-brained bureaucrat, new-found talent, half-crazy, slow-moving*). It's just a matter of becoming consistent.

✏ Adverb-participle modifying phrases are hyphenated unless the adverb ends in *-ly.*

> Well-dressed man, slow-moving traffic, fast-talking salesman
> *(but)*
> Nicely dressed woman, rapidly moving traffic, normally polite boy

✏ Modifying phrases before a noun are seldom hyphenated after it.

> It was a coast-to-coast tour.
> He traveled coast to coast.
> It was word-of-mouth advertising.
> He heard it by word of mouth.

✏ If you use a hyphenated prefix without its modified word (*his pre and post-tournament record; pro and anti-feminism*), you need to add the hyphen just as if the word were there. (*His pre- and post-tournament record, pro- and anti-feminism*).

If the prefix is not hyphenated, you are better off not using it but using two full words instead. And there is no slick way to put the full word first with the hanging prefix following--although it is tried now and then.

> He painted land and seascapes. (*Landscapes and seascapes.*)
> They competed for best-actor and actress honors. (*Best-actor and best-actress honors.*)

IT IS IMPORTANT TO LIMIT
THE NUMBER OF CANDIDATES
SINCE OTHERWISE IT HAS BEEN
ESTIMATED THAT, BEFORE
AN ACQUISITION MAY BE CONCLUDED
OVER 200 CANDIDATES MAY HAVE BEEN
CONSIDERED, WHICH, IN LIGHT OF
THE PROHIBITIVE COST OF REVIEW,
WOULD BE A HIGHLY UNJUSTIFIED
CORPORATE EXPENDITURE.

PUNCTUATION, EVEN PERFECT punctuation, can do only so much. It can't, for example, hold together endless sentences.

I've noticed over the years that compound words tend to shrink. We used to write *saw-toothed, non-committal* and *semi-circle.* Now they are *sawtoothed, noncommittal* and *semicircle.* This may suggest that, when in doubt, leave the hyphen out. I'm not sure.

These pages of guidelines--plus the standard uses required by your organization--should take care of most of your questions. It is enough about punctuation.

If you wish to go further into the subject, I recommend the <u>Washington Post Deskbook on Style.</u> It is readable, well-thought-out and available at your bookstore.

CHAPTER 19

Abbrev.

As a topic, abbreviation probably ranks in interest a tad below yesterday's plant cafeteria menu. But abbreviations have their own set of problems--and uses.

Abbreviations should not only save space and writer's time but also make it easier for the reader to read. Most of them do the first two of these pretty well. But the third goal suffers if the abbreviating is unfamiliar, inconsistent or confusing. A reader would rather read *International Radio-Technical Consortium* than wonder what *IRTC* means.

Most organizations have their own preferences for abbreviations, although they are not likely to be compiled in any one place. Here is a set of guidelines--which I advise you to adjust to conform to your company or agency style.

Four basics:

1. Be consistent in whatever system you use. It is surprisingly easy to become sloppy and vary your style. I fight this constantly.

2. Abbreviate as little as you can. Overabbreviation detracts from clarity and--especially with capital letters--gives your pages a scab-covered look.

That doesn't mean not to abbreviate. The 14th time you write *International Brotherhood of Sarsaparilla Distributors*, it will occur to you there must be a better way.

3. Consider Workarounds. Rather than agonize as to whether to spell out *Institute of Certified Internal Computing Incompetents* or use *ICICI*, consider terms such as *the group, the organization* and *it*.

4. Except with very familiar abbreviations, always spell the words out the first time--and refresh that full spelling every couple of pages; the reader by that time has probably gotten *IDOI* mixed up with *IOID*.

➡ Lowercase and upper-lowercase abbreviations generally take periods: *Corp., c.o.d., d.o.a.* (Exceptions include technical measurements, especially when used with numbers--*2000 rpm, 120 mph.*) All-capitals abbreviations usually do not take periods, except for those describing places: *U.S., N.Y., L.A.,* and academic degrees: *B.S., M.A., Ph.D.*

I SEE ONE-THIRD OF A NATION ILL-HOUSED, ILL-CLAD, ILL-NOURISHED...

...and many people also have faulty toasters and other small appliances.

THE "RULE" AGAINST single-sentence paragraphs is silly. If it had been followed, many of history's best paragraphs would have been watered down by senseless additions. For example, Franklin Roosevelt's Second Inaugural Address.

•◆ Acronyms--words formed from initials--are written in all-caps unless they have become words in their own right, like *radar, laser,* and *scuba.* Use *NATO, DEW line, VISTA.*

•◆ Don't abbreviate a month unless it follows the name of a day of the week. Don't abbreviate any month with five or fewer letters. (You do, too, know which ones they are.)

> We visited them December 12; they returned the visit Monday, Jan. 13.

•◆ Use *a.m.* and *p.m.* Capitalize time zones: *6 a.m. EST.*

•◆ Other than in statistical or tabular matter, you save little space and help the reader little by abbreviating short terms of measurement: *year, hour, mile, meter,* and so on. And often the word beats the abbreviation in name recognition (*18 million barrels,* not *bbls.*)

•◆ Spell *United States* as a noun, abbreviate it *U.S.* as an adjective. Names of government agencies, roads or ships may use the *US* without periods: *USIA, USS Forrestal, US 101.*

•◆ Do not abbreviate US states or provinces, excepting after the name of a city, town or the like. Use zip-code two-letter abbreviations. Don't abbreviate foreign countries; some of them are hard enough to recognize even spelled out. Don't abbreviate cities anywhere.

•◆ Follow standard geographical names. It is not *Ft. Myers, Ft. Worth* or *St. Louis.*

•◆ Don't abbreviate *Avenue* or *Street* except in complete addresses.

> They built on Sepakonka Avenue. Their address will be 2330
> SW Sepakonka Ave., Corbin, N.C.

•◆ Abbreviate any organization whose short version is more familiar than the full spelling.

> IBM, NBC, AFL-CIO, NFL, PTA

For others, spell the name out the first time and parenthesize the abbreviation.

•◆ Some other abbreviations also have become part of the language and are as familiar as, or more familiar than, the original words. Use them, unless you feel it verges on slang:

> AWOL, GI, IOU, MP, POW, TB, TNT, SOS, TV

➥ Use the abbreviations *Co., Corp., Inc.,* but spell out *bureau, department, division, and association*--partly since they don't abbreviate gracefully: *bur, dept, div,* and *assn.*

➥ Spell out *President, Governor, Senator* preceding their full names; it is optional to abbreviate before surnames: *Gov. Cuomo., Sen. D'Amato.*

➥ Use the abbreviations *Dr.* and *Prof.* preceding full names.

➥ Do not abbreviate *attorney general, commandant, detective, superintendent, secretary,* or *secretary general*--or, despite the temptation, *district attorney.*

➥ Abbreviate names of colleges and universities (*UCLA, NYU,* and any well-known local institution--but not *ODCWD,* which if it existed might mean *Obscurity Dental College of West Dakota;* abbreviate that one only if it is less than two miles away).

This short list should give you a core around which to build a style guide that meets your organization's needs.

Whenever in doubt, you'll never go wrong using the full spelling.

CHAPTER 20

Sexist? Not me, Baby!

It is of little help, when accused of sexist language, to say honestly, "I didn't mean nuthin' by it." If someone sees your words as sexist, the harm is done.

The idea is that, if you use masculine and feminine words in certain fixed ways, they reinforce stereotyped views of men and women that our society is trying to change.

For this reason:

> If an employee has a problem, he should see his manager.

should instead be written:

> If an employee has a problem, he or she should see the manager.
> (*or*)
> An employee with a problem should see the manager.

The above example can hardly be seen as creating a stereotype. But if every reference to a manager says *he*, together they do suggest a stereotype: that all (or most) managers are male.

More damaging is the use of *he* in only positive ways:

> As the boss views his automated office...

> The engineer is seen at his workbench.

> The notice tells the homeowner that his taxes will increase.

The damage is that such usage carries on the idea that women seldom if ever hold important jobs or own homes.

So, whereas the generic use of *he* to mean *he or she* used to be convenient but okay, it is now convenient but not okay. It can be worse than that; in a lawsuit alleging sexual discrimination, documents with only *he*'s in them could be used as evidence of bias.

Careful writing (and careful talking, too, when you represent your organization) ought to avoid sexist-sounding language.

Here are some examples, gathered from here and there:

> Every manager should check his file of April issues.

> Today's bright young accounting graduate has his eyes on the challenges...

> I ask the leader of each nation to convey to his people...

Instead of *his*, you have several choices. I recommend mixing them, since each has disadvantages:

1. Change *he* (or *she*) to *he* or *she*.

This is easy to do, requires no restructuring of the sentence, and allows an easy shift to *she or he*, so the male isn't always given top billing.

One disadvantage is that, referring to more than one person, it can get mighty confusing:

> If he or she tells his or her supervisor that he or she is not particularly good at communicating in front of a group unless he or she is the main speaker...

Also, using *he or she* when you know you are discussing only males is silly. If your Boiler Room crew has three supervisors--Bob, Oscar and John-- by all means use *he*. (But not if you are recruiting a fourth supervisor; then describe the supervisory duties as *his or her* responsibilities. The new hire may be Mildred.)

2. Pluralize *he* or *she*. Make it *their*.

> The employee who applies himself to his work.
> (*becomes*)
> Employees who apply themselves to their work.

Again, there are some disadvantages. Among them, pluralizing requires a bit of grammatical care to make it work out.

First, you must pluralize whatever the *their* refers to. It won't do just to pluralize the pronoun and leave singular the thing referred to. Writers often give that a try. It looks like the dickens.

> Make a brief note about the person and their background.

> Have each manager prorate their time.

> Discussions between the employee and their direct supervisor...

> A large measure of an engineer's success is their participation in the project planning process.

What's more, the *their*, when referring to a subject, must modify something plural. It's not enough to change:

> The typical manager is afraid to thumb their nose at
> federal regulations.
> (*to*)
> Typical managers are afraid to thumb their nose at
> federal regulations.

Unless they share a nose, it has to be:

> Typical managers are afraid to thumb their noses at federal
> regulations

One manager, one nose. Two managers, two noses. A fussy grammatical point? Perhaps. An arbitrary one? Not at all.

> The secretaries brought their mothers to the Open House.
> (*Several mothers attended.*)
> The secretaries brought their mother to the Open House.
> (*She was the mama of them all.*)

3. Alternate using *he* and *she*.

This is probably the best long-term solution. (You may want to use *he* in one paragraph or chapter, *she* in another.)

> (*All from the same article:*)
> The visitor who finds herself confused by street signs....
>
> If a pedestrian were to lose his way in the Village...
>
> The magazine will appeal to the resident who prefers her news in
> capsule form...

There is a disadvantage: You can sometimes become careless.

> Even the secretary who respects her boss may still be annoyed
> when he smokes in the office.

The implication there is that secretaries are always women, bosses always men.

4. Rewrite the sentence so no *he* or *she* is needed.

> The typical state agency manager has 10 years service to his credit.
> (*Try instead*)
> The typical state agency manager has 10 years service.
> (*or*)
> The typical state agency manager is credited with 10 years service.

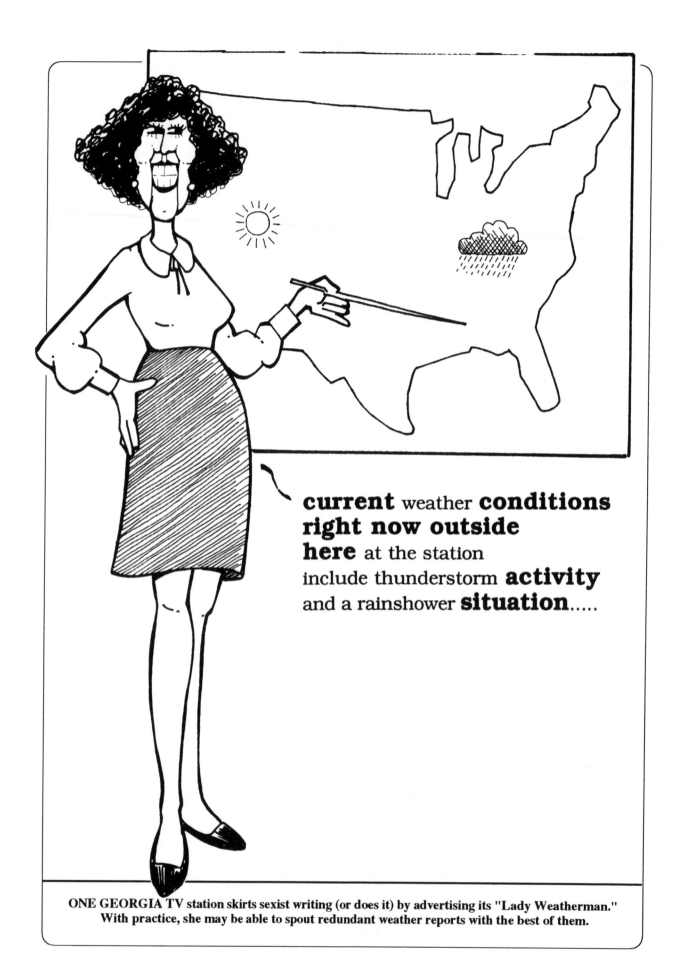

current weather **conditions**
right now outside
here at the station
include thunderstorm **activity**
and a rainshower **situation**.....

ONE GEORGIA TV station skirts sexist writing (or does it) by advertising its "Lady Weatherman."
With practice, she may be able to spout redundant weather reports with the best of them.

A technical director, when he considers the increase in forms,...
(Try instead)
A technical director, when considering the increase in forms,....
(or)
When a technical director considers the increase in forms,....

5. Use you instead of *he* or *she*.

It's legal to ask the applicant what he seeks in the way of a career.
(becomes)
It's legal to ask the applicant, "What do you seek in the way
of a career?"

Other words than pronouns can suggest certain stereotyped ideas; among them, that certain jobs are male, certain ones female. Here are a few of those words:

Watchman, busboy, stewardess, chairman, manpower,
stationmaster, policeman.

Some such words may certainly be used without taint of sexism:

Penmanship, first baseman, manhole, freshman.

Many suggested substitutes are as accurate and appropriate as the words they replace. *Guard* neatly replaces *watchman,* so you can avoid clumsy terms like *watchperson* or *lady watchman.* And *work force* in most instances replaces *manpower.*

But other substitutes suggested, even by reputable books on non-sexist writing, sound not only foggy but also inaccurate. For instance, *dining room attendant* has been suggested instead of *busboy.* Come on...how would that sound?

The Johnsons' lazy son Homer has a part-time job as dining-room
attendant at Slug's Greasy Spoon Diner.

Substitutes should never sound silly, or they'll defeat the purpose of non-sexist writing by seeming to make fun of it.

For instance, the same guidebook suggests replacing *widow* and *widower* with the generic term *surviving spouse.* I see little point in that.

In the first place, it is no stereotype to call a widow a widow; widows will always be women. Nor is it a derogatory term that suggests something inferior to widower (in the way that *stewardess* does imply a possibly inferior mini-version of *steward).*

201

Third, *surviving spouse* certainly has limited usefulness, largely in legal or formal contexts. Otherwise it can sound silly: *Uncle Milford went and got married to a cute little surviving spouse from Waldport.*

So, always use perspective and judgment. George Orwell advised writers: Break any rule rather than write something barbarous.

Some stray questions and answers:

<u>Is it all right to use the words *girl* or *gal?*</u>

Use them only when you would as naturally say *boy* or *guy.* That means almost always in conversational, rather than written, messages. ("Some of the guys in the work crew...")

<u>How about *ladies?*</u>

Use *ladies* when you would as naturally use *gentlemen.* That means largely in formal or festive occasions.

<u>Is the word *female* acceptable?</u>

As a modifier (*female employees*) it may have some usefulness. But as a noun (*34 females on the staff*), it sounds impersonal and legalistic. Any female person old enough to hold a job is a woman.

<u>How do you write a salutation in a letter when you don't know whether a man or woman will read it?</u>

It's acceptable to leave the salutation off. Or you can comfortably address the job title (*Dear Director Walton*) or the agency or department (*Dear Customer Service*).

In all cases, avoid abominations such as *To whom it may concern:*

Although we should always watch for its lingering signs, racially biased writing has pretty much vanished.

A more likely characteristic of racist (and sexist) writing is the use of awkward legalistic wording. It's always wise to be direct and natural rather than stuffily bureaucratic. Even for stuffy bureaucrats.

For instance, a company's EEO compliance report notes that recent staff additions included *one female minority.*

Is that somehow an improvement over *one black woman?*

SOME READING I'VE LIKED

Someone said, and many teachers have repeated, that you learn to write by writing. So you do. But you can learn about writing by reading good writing—and good books on writing. Here are a few I recommend:

If You Want to Write, by Brenda Ueland; Graywolf Press. Ms. Ueland, a contemporary of Eugene O'Neill, has been "rediscovered" in recent years. We ought all be thankful. Her book has almost nothing to do with writing on the job, but everything to do with *writing.* Subtitled "A Book About Art, Independence and Spirit," it is even more than that. It is a book of inspiration. If you want to write, this small book is must reading. Carl Sandburg considered it "The best book ever written about how to write."

Writer's Guide and Index to Literature, by Porter Perrin; Scott, Foresman and Company. You may have trouble rousting out a copy of this great college handbook, last published in 1943. It is my favorite. He deals in a scholarly, most thorough way with matters of correctness, style and clear thinking. Dr. Perrin comes through as helpful and wise. I wish I had had him as a teacher. In a sense, through his fine book, I have.

The Careful Writer, by Theodore Bernstein; Atheneum. Mr. Bernstein, newsman and teacher, covers enormous ground here. He preaches clarity and thoughtful writing, and practices it, too, in his large, informative and often witty guidebook. His eye for language foibles equals that of Edwin Newman; but, unlike Newman, he does not skewer the writer while analyzing the writing.

Look It Up, Rudolf Flesch; Harper & Row. Mr. Flesch, probably the most noted champion of Plain English, deviates here from his narrative books to provide a concise and comprehensive "deskbook of style and usage." He intended to make it useful and reliable. It is both. But it is not a book to sit on the shelf. As the author—sometimes a bit of a scold—writes: "It won't do you any good if you don't do what the title says—look it up."

And you can't go wrong reading *The Complete Plain Words,* by Sir Ernest Gowers, Pelican Books; *The Elements of Style,* by E. B. White (who credits also his mentor, William Strunk Jr.), MacMillan Publishing Company; *Writing With Style,* by Peter Jacobi, Lawrence Ragan Communications, or *On Writing Well,* by William Zinsser, Harper and Row. I re-read each of these often.

Mr. Zinsser's book is almost unique in that it includes a discussion of humor. And he knows what he's talking about. His "Annual Reprot" (his misspelling is deliberate), a short book satirizing shareholder letters, is rib-bustingly funny.

Off the beaten track, there are many excellent books with highly specific thrusts. I think you'll find delightful and idea-provoking these four books:

The Transitive Vampire; A Handbook of Grammar for the Innocent, the Eager and the Doomed, by Karen Elizabeth Gordon, Times Books; *Diagrams, a Visual Survey of Graphs, Maps and Charts,* by Arthur Lockwood, Watson-Guptill; *Lateral Thinking; a Handbook for Creativity* by Edward DeBono, American Management Association; and *My Years With Ross,* James Thurber, Simon & Schuster.

Anything by E. B. White; anything by Roger Rosenblatt; almost anything by George Will; anything by Abraham Lincoln. And, to keep your sanity in a tumultuous world, an occasional large dollup of Robert Benchley, who squoze* more humor into fewer words than anyone before or since.

*No, Virginia, there is no such word.

INDEX

WHY LEARN WRITING PRINCIPLES?

High school and college students, as well as adults, often lose sight of the answer. They think using long sentences and big words will impress a teacher or professor, the boss, or even close friends.

But when you think about it, there are only three essential objectives in writing:

- To be readable.
  If writing is awkward, stiff, or full of mistakes, readers quit.

- To be understood.
  Readers must get what's being said.

- To move someone to action.
  Exceptional writing makes the reader laugh, cry, pray, form an opinion or change one, vote, demonstrate, or march off to war.

How does learning grammar and usage relate to the three objectives? Simple. Without tools, you can't build a house. Without a saw, hammer, and nails, you won't get far constructing a shed, much less a church. You need tools to accomplish your goal. You need a knowledge of writing principles.

Our book, *Write Smarter, Not Harder*, isn't like other texts. For one thing, it's entertaining, and that makes learning fun. But, more than that, it focuses on what one really needs to know to write well. With *Write Smarter, Not Harder*, you'll teach your teenager to master the principles of grammar and usage to make writing:

1. concise
2. organized
3. persuasive

1. **Readability. Being concise.**
   Great writers possess two traits: their ideas average eighteen words per sentence, and no more than five percent of their words are three syllables or more.

   Write Smarter, Not Harder will show you how to test any piece of writing for clarity and conciseness. Are the sentences too long, or the words too heavy? If your teenager's writing isn't readable, steer it in a new direction — conciseness. The text explains how to cut extraneous words. It also gives four legitimate reasons for big words and shows you when to use them and when not to.

2. Being understood. Learning to organize.

The worst advice for organizing is, "Just get it down on paper. Then go back and polish." "Letting it flow" is guaranteed to muddle ideas and doom your writing.

Write Smarter, Not Harder shows you how to capture ideas separately from writing and why it's critical to do so. Rough drafts create awkward sequences and problems of omission and redundancy. But worse, "just getting it down" adds unnecessary stress. Our approach to organizing ideas eliminates writer's block and contributes to coherent, clear thought.

3. Persuasion. Discover the power of verbs.

Words are powerful. Sticks and stones may break your bones, but words can break your heart, open your mind, or save your soul. If writing doesn't convince, it fails. It doesn't matter that it was readable. Good writing promotes action.

Write Smarter, Not Harder teaches you how to utilize these powerful atoms, verbs, which drive persuasive sentences. Writing that uses precise verbs earns better grades, gets a job, or secures a promotion.

If you understand verbs, you'll eliminate ninety percent of your writing problems.

Consider these sentences:
- The parents discussed the problem.
- The problem was discussed by the parents.
- The parents gave a discussion of the problem.
- A discussion of the problem was given by the parents.

Is there any difference in *meaning* among the four sentences? No, they mean the same. Then, what *is* the difference among them? Why is the last sentence double the length of the first one? Why are the last three sentences less concise and understandable? Because the verbs are handled in a clumsy manner. Verb skill makes or breaks the writer, especially a college-bound teenager interested in career advancement.

Summary

Write Smarter, Not Harder makes the writing process fun, logical, natural, and manageable. Writing doesn't have to be a mysterious, frustrating, or miserable task. With our text, teenagers can improve their skills and profit in college or on the job. The lessons are easy to grasp, and your writing will become concise, organized, and persuasive.

Move ahead. Write smarter, not harder!

FOR THE TEACHER/PARENT OR TEENAGER
Hardback, 231 pages
$35 includes shipping

TEACHING THE BEGINNING WRITER

Now your older child has seen the value of **ENOUGH ABOUT GRAMMAR**, we'd like to encourage you to help your younger children learn to enjoy writing, too. Most children find writing difficult, or worse, **B-O-R-I-N-G**, and I don't blame them!

What a shame, though, because writing is one of the most important tasks we do.

- It's a key to later success in school (essays, tests).
- We communicate mostly through spoken and written language.
- Other people interpret us through what we write (letters, postcards).
- It's a way for us to have fun and give pleasure (biographies, stories).

Without writing we'd be lost. So it's sad young children find writing so painful to learn. Children rarely envision writing as creative or vital.

But there's hope. In an exciting, **short** hour, I'll show you how to change your children's minds about writing. You can make writing fun and teach them a skill that will enhance their creative ability.

WHY WRITING TURNS KIDS OFF

In most schooling learning grammar requires memorizing lots of definitions and rules. Children start by wrestling with the elements of a sentence — noun, verb, adjective, adverb, subject, predicate, etc. Then they're pinned down to the drudgery of diagramming sentences and a dizzying complexity of grammatical constructions.

No wonder writing turns kids off. None of this touches the fun part of learning.

TURNING KIDS ON

Wouldn't you like to push a special button that would make your children like to write — a button that would change drab, stilted writing into concise, lively, colorful prose? Well, such a button really exists. Your children can make every sentence dance, sing, or shout.

How? Children overuse *is, are, were, have, has* and *had*. You can see it in almost every sentence a child writes: "My name is Jessica. I am seven. I have a puppy. He is bad."

But once a child catches on to verbs, the writing livens up. Isn't writing "My puppy growls, scratches, claws, drools, wets, paws, bites, or barks" much more fun than writing "My puppy is bad?"

Besides, "My dog is bad" **ends** the story, whereas any of the other verbs nudges the child to other ideas. Who was bitten? Why? What did the puppy paw at or drool on? What were the consequences? The story goes on.

Verb skill makes or breaks a writer, whether an adult or a child. Great writers know the value of strong verbs.

- "Forgive us our sins," <u>not</u> "We hope you will forgive our sins."
- "Call me Ishmael," <u>not</u> "My name is Ishmael."
- "Jesus wept," <u>not</u> "Jesus had an experience of crying."

Undermining the verb leads to wordiness and increases the chance of grammatical errors. Using verbs correctly automatically drives concise, lively, persuasive writing.

THE SELLING PART

We offer a new book, guides and a video that will **immediately** plug your child into the fun, creative side of writing. The package contains four parts:

1. *Jessica's Journeys* — A hardback, four-color, heavily illustrated children's book which describes a compelling adventure similar to the C.S. Lewis *Narnia* series.

2. <u>A Teacher's Guide</u> — Shows parents how to lead children through learning verbs.

3. <u>Student Workbook</u> — Exercises that teach children exactly what drives language, what persuades and how to spark the reader's interest.

4. <u>Video and text</u> — A **humorous** film that shows parents why verbs are the most critical part of writing. The text and workbook confirm how verbs intensify imagery, conciseness and persuasion.

This package benefits the 4-year-old to the 40-year-old. The toddler will love *Jessica's Journeys* simply as a compelling story with its rich illustrations. Using the guides, the beginning writer will start to master the part of writing that's fun. From the video, the parent/ teacher or teenager will suddenly realize what it takes to persuade, to change opinions, to move a heart, or to save a soul.

The pen is mightier than the sword but only if one knows how to wield the pen. In a short, exciting hour your child will learn the fun, creative side of writing.

Naturally, I guarantee everything I've said. We've taken ten years to create this unique package, so we want to give a unique guarantee. Your check **won't be cashed for 30 days**. Order whatever part of the package you want, look it over and decide whether or not to keep it. If you're not one hundred percent pleased, return the material, and your **uncashed** check will be returned **immediately.**

Check off your request:

- [ ] $35   Verb Skills Package
  - *Jessica's Journeys*
  - Parent's Guide and answer key
  - Student Workbook

- [ ] $35   Video - *Driving It Home;* text, workbook, and answer key

- [ ] $50   Both of the above (save $20)

$_____   Subtotal ($35 or $50)

- [ ] $5   Shipping, Insurance

$_____   Total enclosed ($40 or $55)

- [ ] $35 ($30 plus $5 shipping) *Write Smarter, Not Harder*

(Credit cards are not accepted because cards increase the cost.)

Guarantee: Your check will not be cashed for 30 days. If you're not one hundred percent satisfied, return the package, and your uncashed check will be returned immediately.

_____
Name (please print)

_____
Street Address (not P.O. Box) (please print)

_____
City (please print)   State   Zip

Twain Publishers • 2120 Timberlane • Wheaton, IL 60187 • 630-665-9370

NOTES

NOTES

NOTES

NOTES

NOTES

NOTES